SOMETHING'S ALWAYS HAPPENING:
Reflections on a Blessed Life

by Mark Baxter

With Melissa Dickson Jackson

PSALM 19: 1-6

1
The heavens declare the glory of God;
the skies proclaim the work of his hands.

2
Day after day they pour forth speech;
night after night they reveal knowledge.

3
They have no speech, they use no words;
no sound is heard from them.

4
Yet their voice goes out into all the earth,
their words to the ends of the world.
In the heavens God has pitched a tent for the sun.

5
It is like a bridegroom coming out of his chamber,
like a champion rejoicing to run his course.

6
It rises at one end of the heavens
and makes its circuit to the other;
nothing is deprived of its warmth.

Table of Contents

7

NOTE FROM THE AUTHOR

This journal started some years back. I think the desire, the need, the seed, started when I tried to write a letter to my fourth-grade teacher's husband. I really wanted to, and I tried, but to no success. Then came my daughter, Toot, a few years later with a book to write down life stories. I didn't like the questions in the book, but I loved that Katherine wanted to know some of my life stories. My inspiration was my Tootie-Bell. I would have to try to learn to write.

Somehow, I heard about the University of West Georgia's free admission for senior citizens. I went down and signed up and so started my journey in writing. I wasn't really thinking I would be able to write, but I thought it might be fun, and I had the time, AND it was free. I'd give it a try. Maybe a couple of stories would come out — at least one about my *Toot*.

So, in comes my writing professor, tutor, and teacher, Mrs. Jackson. It started with a fall class of kids — I could be their great grandfather. I remember the kids in the class would ask questions of Mrs. Jackson, and Mrs. Jackson would answer them. She would enlighten them. I was impressed. And I always have questions. It's in my nature. It's how I learn. I'd be up at the end of the class asking questions, too — very enlightening and kind answers. But one day, I asked Mrs. Jackson about something, and I tried to convey that I knew something about writing. Mrs. Jackson told me in a very nice tone, "I'm the teacher and you're the student." THAT was the beginning of my writing and learning how.

I think after that encounter, she gave me a writing journal. In the front she had written,

What's important Here:
Memories, Ideas, Inspirations, Visions.

Not Important Here:
Spelling, Grammar, Punctuation, Handwriting.

These truths were the start to unlock the stories I wanted to tell for my *Toot*. This was the start. I could see this might be possible. That maybe I could write a few stories with the help, guidance, encouragement, wisdom, and patience of Mrs. Jackson this would be possible. I did not realize how many stories I had locked up in storage, in my head. It was like a floodgate. They just started coming. Here are a few of them written down.

As I look back, this has been a very emotional trip at times. Sometimes I wonder, how does Mrs. Jackson put up with me? As I think over my life through these stories and the feelings that accompany them, I can see the truth of God's word in Psalm 23, "Surely Goodness and mercy will follow me all the days of my life." And it has.

Mark Baxter
Jan 18, 2024

SOMETHING'S ALWAYS HAPPENING
ON THE POND

1.   Every evening the swallows come when it's getting dark, grabbing bugs. Then when it gets a little darker the bats come.

2.   The progression with life in the foliage, spring and fall, always changing.

3.   Pollywogs in every stage of life.

4.   Caterpillars and cocoons on the side of the pond falling in. Fish gathering to eat them.

5.   The wasp pods finding places to stay.

6.   The colors of the leaves.

7.   The delicate beauty of each new flower.

8.   Beavers—they are everywhere that there is water. They are great builders and woodsmen, and they don't like us to interfere.

9.   I don't get tired of seeing their woodwork and dams.

10.   I don't believe the beavers can do what they do.

11.   Wild white lilies on the hillside— I never would have seen them if I didn't go out to the pond.

MORNING FISHING TRIP

I always say the morning is the best time to go fishing. The morning—a new day! A new beginning! The sun is just coming up. The dew. The smells. The anticipation. It's hard to get up so early, but I've got a fishing plan with a new friend, Dave. On mornings like this, I usually get up many times before it's time to go because I don't want to miss my appointment. I said I would be there. Got to go. Don't be late.

I made it on time. It was a beautiful morning. I met Dave at Little Giant. He had a spot not too far away to take me fishing. I was looking forward to it. We head off in his rig with fishing poles and tackle.

We pull into a nice-looking pond, gleaming in the morning sun. It was wooded on one side and partially wooded on the other side. Dave was the first one in the water. He had two nice fish before I could get going. I thought I should head down along the pond on the wooded side.

It had a pathway or deer trail along the water. It was nice. I made a few casts when there was an opening in the wood line. I caught one, and decided to move down. A pine tree about two feet in diameter had fallen across the ravine along the trail. I'd have to get past that first, so I walked around it to find my next spot in the pond.

I caught another, and I started to really enjoy being along the trail in the morning. Colors seem brighter. I was getting taken in by it all. A bullfrog jumped by me. I caught another bass. I had another one on. I thought it was a big one. It got off and made a big swirl in the water. I could hear the traffic going by in the distance. What a contrast that was.

There were a lot of pricker bushes around the pond. I wonder why God made those. They just seem to tangle you up when you go through the woods, and sometimes they stick you. Kinda like life, I guess — maybe it's a reminder. I have a pair of scissors, and I cut them back. I need a bigger set of those. I always say that every time I use them.

I was getting close to this end of the pond. It's swampy, and I can't make it around. Well at least I did one side. I'm heading back, refreshed and pleased. Built up, spirits lifted, and I'm a little surprised.

This time when I get to the felled pine tree, I climb on top of it and cross the ravine tightrope style instead of walking around it and head back up the trail to meet Dave.

IT'S MORE THAN FISHING

There are things that are happening in and along
waterways, wooded areas, the highways and byways of life
that you experience when you are out there fishing. It's in
the doing. I've been thinking about these things that
happen when I go fishing lately:

Seeing muskrats going along the water's edge within inches
    of you when you're in waders

The work they do to keep the phragmites back from the
    water's edge

The barn swallows that show up in the evening going
    around the pond looking for bugs

The bats that come out after dark darting around after
    bugs

The gathering of barn swallows in fall, thousands of them,
    preparing to go south

Beavers and the work they do: tree chopping and building.
    Hard to believe. They are everywhere the water
    runs

The cormorants nesting in bushes on the pond — When I
    make my way around the pond on my tip toes in
    my waders, they let out a screeching sound that
    could give you a heart attack

The milkweed growing and shedding — what a mess it is,
    millions of seeds

The black bear working its way around the shoreline. He
    didn't see us. How startlingly black he was

The small islands that form in the West Branch of Upstate
    New York — When the water lowers the
    wildflowers rage big and beautiful in pinks and
    yellows until they disappear under the waterline
    again

The mating of snapping turtles within two feet of me in
    my waders at Cove Pond

The run of Blue Gills from one pond to another in the fall

The owls mating in trees in the springtime on Great Pond

The white tulip-like flowers covering the wooded hillside
    in Spring at Lake Redwine

The setting of the sun in Fall makes landmarks appear so
    different, almost unrecognizable

To see in a real way why it's not good for wild animals to
    lose their fear of man

Just to see how much is going on in nature — the darning
    needles landing on the end of the fishing pole

The caterpillars nesting in trees that fall out in the autumn
    and the fish waiting to feed on them

The abundance of life in ponds, especially bug life

The spiders who reside in cattails and how they swing out
    in the water to a single cattail

How vultures and maggots can pick a deer clean in a
    matter of days

How the fish will eat the maggots that fall off the carcass
    at the water's edge

The evening when we were fishing at Kenny's Pond and
thousands of toads moved out from the bushes
into the roadway — thousands! They were all
along the ramp area and the road access. It was
hard to pull out without running over several of
them.

The frog that ate a Gary Yamamoto worm off the end of
my line at Secret Pond in late summer

The porcupine my son Tom scared up and chased through
the woods in the Catskills when he was 16

The time going down the Delaware River fishing and
seeing the beautiful bends and turns and scenery
in the river, and there's no one there but you

The beautiful ground covers — grass growing solidly on
drying pond sides — how quickly it becomes lush
and green

Seeing the field of lily pads being eaten by Beavers

Turtles eating frogs

Frogs eating insects

The trout trying to jump over the waterfalls, even
waterfalls ten-feet tall

The purple passion fruit and its vine

The coloring in fall

The crackling of leaves under your feet

The flowering of plant life at all times of the year

These are some of the reasons to go fishing. It is an adventure every trip — life in every stage and the nature of nature, the marvel of how much is going on at all times, and all you need to do is pay attention to see it and to realize that we only see a small bit of the miracle going on all around us every day. The creation is so marvelous; the more you look, the more marvelous it is. God does not disappoint.

1953 INTERNATIONAL DUMP TRUCK: HUMBLE BEGINNINGS

It's the fourth of July weekend, and I've been thinking about beginnings and America and what a great country it is — all the opportunity that is here for all those that want to work hard. My story starts with working hard, a gift that I believe I was born with. I didn't realize it until I got older. I haven't always used that gift properly. But this story is about America and the opportunities here. It starts with coming back from the Army and trying to get some work. I used some of my skills to work and make a living. I wasn't a believer at the time, but as I look back, God's hand, goodness, and mercy was on me. This story starts with looking for a truck that dumped, a dump truck.

I was doing clean up jobs and had some tree work. I remember passing Smith's Auto Sales on Sunrise Highway in Babylon, NY. They had a dump truck on the lot. All the vehicles were used. The truck came from the Shelter Island Oyster Company. It had 17,000 miles on it. That was in 1975. It ran really nice. It had a two-speed rear. I remember that the five-ton dump truck in the Army had a two-speed rear also. It had a steel dump bed. I think it was $500. I bought it. I got to be a friend of the Smith

Auto Sales people and did some work for them, so I was set to do more tree work and clean-up work.

The work came in through word-of-mouth. Just being out there working, I got more work. One day, I got a job doing clean up off Albany Ave for a retired New York City detective. Albany Ave in the 1970s was a kinda scary place. He owned some rental houses, not in a good neighborhood and not in good shape. I can't remember how I got him as a customer, probably I was cheaper than the other guys, and I worked hard. I think he owned a few on the same street. There was lots of junk and trash around.

One day, I was cleaning up the debris and trash in one yard, and I went to the next house. The lady living there was a girl I went to school with who was in a lot of my classes and was very smart. I felt bad for her living there. I remember going down into the basement with the owner. I noticed a leak in the bathroom wall, and I said to him, I can fix that. They had turned the water off. I had some skills that I had learned from my dad, and John Sunderland who I had worked for when I was a kid. My family had been in the plumbing business for four generations. I had no tools — no plumbing tools, for sure! But I got some. I resoldered the piping, and I got that dear lady's plumbing back online. From then on, I would carry plumbing tools in the door of the 1953 International Dump truck.

That was the start of a fifty-year career that's still on going. I was talking to a young man at church. He's working on becoming a plumber. He's doing side work out of a motorcycle. In America, with hard work and the grace of God, blessings come.

We just don't know the future, but with diligence and the grace of God, a lot can happen.

RESTLESS:
HOW I DISCOVERED PECONIC LODGE AND THE NORTH FORK OF LONG ISLAND

I've wanted to live in the country, really, all my life. I think back to working hard and building forts in my backyard. I built many of them and learned how to work in my backyard with a handsaw, nails, and a hammer as my tools. I was, and still am, a country boy at heart. I wanted to be in the country, so after I got out of the military, I was looking around for a place to get away from it all and back to nature. I wanted space around. This is the short version of my effort to accomplish that.

The International Dump Truck and its origins inspired me to go check out Shelter Island where the truck had been used by the Shelter Island Oyster Company. I thought I would take a ride out there in the dump truck. I think it only went 55 mph, but we made it. Jacki and I motored over to Shelter Island on a ferry boat. It was a really beautiful ride with stunning scenery. It's like a break from the everyday — to be on a boat with your car, in this case, your dump truck.

When we exited the ferry, I had the feeling that the truck felt at home there on the island. We came in through the small town with about five stores and very little traffic and headed up the hill then made a right on Shore Road, Highway 115. It took us to the beach that ran parallel to the road. It must have been late in the day because I decided that we needed a place to stay.

There were three old wooden structures that ran along 115. It was an old girl scout camp that had been converted to a vacation lodge. It had the look of a camp or barracks. It had some small cottages and rooms, and a big kitchen in a separate building. I remember the old gent running the place with his wife, daughter, and son-in-law. His name was Mr. Hammer. He sized me up, and he did it in a nice way. He didn't want any trouble in his place. The dump truck didn't scare him off. I passed his inspection.

I bet not too many people came here to stay driving a '53 International dump truck. We got along, me and Mr. Hammer. We stayed in one of his cottages. It was a fun experience. We returned many times after that. I remember going home the next day and looking around at all the farms and open land. This was far enough away to *get away*. It was a beautiful spot, this north fork of Long Island.

Some years later, after Jacki and I married, we found our own place out there.

GROWING UP: TASSELS AND SIGNS

I remember some years back, maybe ten years ago or so, I'm not sure why it came to me, but it was in a moment in time that I was thinking "my children are grown up and can take care of themselves." It was a good feeling. I'm not sure *feeling* is the right word but considering all the evil things and pitfalls around us and remembering the holes that their father fell in on his growing up, I was proud of my children and the successes that their hard work has brought them through the grace of God and prayer. When it comes to raising a child up in the way they should go, I didn't really have a gauge to look at except the scriptures. They aren't born from above, but there is still hope. We pray for that all the time. So, these thoughts bring me to this photo of my dad and this story.

As I was looking through the old pictures, this one came up: my dad standing in front of the Mark Baxter Heating and Plumbing sign in my yard on Route 110 in Amityville, NY. It was along the same lane that my grandfather walked daily from his home and shop into town where he was a trustee and community leader.

The property had been the Powell Moving Company's which started around the turn of the century. The Powell building caught on fire and burnt down a big wooden structure. It was a heck of a blaze. The charcoal chips from that fire were as big as a folded newspaper as they floated through the air. It's a miracle nothing else caught on fire. There's a lot of history there.

A couple of years later, I bought the lot and used it as my equipment yard. It took a lot of work and God's Grace to get to this point in my plumbing career. Just a year or two later, I moved to North Fork and set up business there.

My dad used to collect the tassels from our graduation caps, and it would be the tassels that he hung above his desk. He had a special spot for them. He had six kids, so he had six tassels. I know that he took pride in them and thought that his job was finished when his kids graduated from High School and handed him the tassel.

I'm really happy that I have this picture of Dad leaning into my sign, his hand raised high and gripping the post. I can still see the pride in his eyes, the relief that I could truly take care of myself. It really speaks to me. That sign — it was more than just a tassel.

DIVINE APPOINTMENTS

All of life I believe is a divine appointment. Most of the time we just don't see it or really understand that God is directing all things according to his will for his own glory. I had a visible and believable divine appointment yesterday evening.

I had bought a kit for the barbeque grill to redo the ignition of the gas grill which did not work properly. It was supposed to come with all the parts including ignitor wires and spark igniters. It only came with the ignitor. I was going to send it back and order it again, but I decided to go get a connector at Lowes and put it back together myself. I didn't want to do this, but I wanted to get it working, so off to Lowes in the evening I go.

As I'm going in the exit door of Lowes, I see a fellow with an old blue water tank in the cart. It looked familiar, and he looked familiar. His son recognized me, and I him. It was a family from church that I had helped with a water heater a few weeks back. He was in Lowes with the boys because he couldn't get a broken fitting out of the expansion tank. I was able to guide him and give him some info about getting it out and also putting a drain in the line so he wouldn't have to lift the cover which started the problem in the first place.

I got to talk to his sons. He showed me a picture of his little girl that had helped with the water heater. She was in the crawl space with me and her dad. I really appreciated her standing upright as her dad and I were on our hands and knees. She stood there silhouetted in the light of the crawl space door with her hair poking out around her head and light reflecting off her glasses and her smile. It was a beautiful sight. Funny how God brings moments like that into our lives. It was a difficult job, but a beautiful experience. It's surprising that amidst those struggles, there is joy you can take away.

So, if it wasn't for them sending me a kit with missing parts for my grill, I would not have been at Lowes that night to see them again and remember the ways that God blesses us even in the moments of frustration and challenge. Lowes didn't even have the part I needed, but now I realize, God sent me for other reasons.

BRINGING THE BOAT AROUND

It was time to get my ten-foot John boat that the boys and I fished out of for many years, a nice little, lite boat. Tom's in-laws bought a house on Lake Kedron in Peachtree City, a 220-acre lake. It's a nice lake, all natural with no docks, but you can leave small crafts in the woods and drag them down to the water. So, I head to Moreland, GA, to pick up the John Boat about thirty minutes south of here. I'm driving my old 2004 E-350 Econoline Van, a good match for the John Boat. It fits in the back with the door closed. I've been on a lot of trips that way, mostly in New York. So, I'm off. It kind of felt nice driving the old Ford Van. I haven't used it much of late, since I got the new Ford Pickup which I'm starting to like.

It takes about a half hour to get to Moreland. It's a nice place. I pull into Tyler's where the boat is and turn around so the truck back is in the right position to load the boat. Tyler gets out his tractor and he pulls the boat up from the pond to the back of the truck. I loaded up the boat but then I couldn't put the van in reverse, so I had to drive forward.

I get out on the highway, and it would only drive in low gear. I thought I would go to Peachtree City and unload the boat. I was headed that way, but realized it wasn't a good idea, and turned around and headed home. My top speed was 25, really more like 20. I must have pulled over half-a-dozen times to let people pass me. I'm stopped a hundred feet from the intersection, and I'm having problems with my GPS, but I know I need HWY 29. The sign here has multiple different roads on it. I'm still debating about going home in first gear. It's like the old days. It's a go, lord help me.

I'm low on gas, and I also need to stop someplace. There's an older gas station on 29 with a convenience store. I pull into the gas station. The tank was on the driver's side, and I pulled into the wrong side. I have to pull out and pull in again. I don't want to turn off the van because it might not start in gear. So, I have the emergency brake on and the truck running in gear at the pumps.

I went to the convenience store to pay for the gas and get an ice tea. A cute little girl, maybe three or four, was there with her mom, the cashier. She had a little brown bag with some artwork, and was looking for tips. She had such a nice smile that I gave her a tip. I go back out to the truck, and finish pumping gas. A lady pulls into the next station over. She has a nice fancy new pickup. She locked her keys in the truck and asked me if I could help, with my truck that only goes in first gear running as I put gas in.

I really wanted to help, and I thought hard about it. When we realize there is a problem, we too often go to God late when really it should be the first thing we do in situations like these. Pray. Cast our cares on him for he cares for us. I go over to the lady, and I ask her if I can pray for her. She says, yes, so I prayed for her. It felt right. She was at peace when I left her. I felt happy.

I take the emergency break off and head home on HWY 29 at 20 mph thinking, *this might be the last adventure in my 2004 Ford van.*

1940 CHRIS CRAFT CABIN CRUISER

Boats—I've always loved boats! My father always
had a boat and would take the family out on it. We did a
lot of clamming in those days. The first boat I remember is
a 16-foot lap-streak wooden boat, open with bench seats
and two small seats in back to steer the boat. That boat
had a 25-horsepower 1950s Evinrude Outboard. I
remember leaving the Amityville Creek going across the
Great South Bay and going over to Gilgo, a trip that we
would make many, many times. It was a beautiful,
picturesque boat ride. As a kid I didn't really appreciate it
the way I do now.

When I was a young boy, we were leaving the
Amityville Creek and I remember thinking "if we sink, I
won't be able to swim that far to shore." It was a little
scary. I had to be about 8-years-old. That was my father's
first boat. He had other bigger ones. That's how boating
goes for many people—you keep getting bigger ones.

It was a boat city out there. I remember when my
father got a bigger boat, the 16-foot-lapstrake boat was
turned upside-down on the last island in the Amityville
River. We saw it there for years when we headed out on
the bay in newer, bigger boats. When we were going out
on the boat, we would look at all the other boats anchored

to the bulkhead and boathouses. We'd talk about them, and I got to *really* like the way they looked, and the way they were built. The mahogany, the brightwork—they really are works of art. I began to dream that I would have such a boat one day.

This started my love affair with boats—going out with my father and listening to him talk about the beauty, form, and craftsmanship of other people's boats. My father would talk about the commitment of the owners and the maintenance of the boats. I remember him saying the phrase "nice shape." It was important to keep your boat in "nice shape." Yep, I was hooked. There was some status to having a big boat, like you made it in America, especially here on the south shore of Long Island where boating and boats are everywhere.

The streets in South Amityville had canals behind the houses, and they all had boats: sailing, outboards, and cabin cruisers with inboard motors. I remember back when I got out of the Service in 1973, I had a job with a small siding company for a few months. I did a small gutter job for a friend of mine, John Bried. He was working in a marina in Oakdale. I believe he was running the boat motor repairs there. I was speaking to him about a cabin cruiser for sale, probably in a dreamy, aspirational kind of way. I was always thinking about boats. As it turned out, there was one for sale at the marina, a 28-foot Chris Craft Cabin Cruiser — 1940, wood, with a flat head six-cylinder. It was thirty-some-odd years old. I think the man wanted $450 dollars. I could do that, I thought.

I needed a place to keep it. I knew someone in South Amityville who might let me keep the boat at his place. I made a deal to paint their house in exchange for keeping the boat at their place. I got two fellows from the firehouse that needed some work, so they painted the house for $400. Here was my dream coming true. A lot of things happened, and I learned a lot, too. I didn't realize then how little I knew and how much I would have to learn.

Some of the nicest times on the water were in that Chris Craft, especially in the evening when the water was like glass, cruising the Great South Bay. There was something magical about going five miles an hour through that glistening water, golden in the evening sun, the smell of the salt-water and the low hum of the motor below the deck. It was breathtaking.

Just thinking about it fifty years later puts a smile on my face. I also learned that I'm a fair-weather sailor. I do not like it when the wind blows and the water is rough. I still say that from time to time: "I'm a fair-weather sailor."

I also learned that boating costs a lot of money, and takes a lot of work. Keeping an eye on your boat must always be on the back of your mind. My father had told me those things, but as a boy, I only saw the beauty and the joy of that glistening water. I had the boat for one long season. I did not sink it. I used it quite a bit, and I'm glad I did. My dad had a friend in town who had a piece of property to put it on. I kept the boat there until I sold it a year later for what I paid for it. My mind had shifted to work and all the obligations that would make way for the family that Jacki and I would have. My father was right; it was a lot of work.

CLAMMING

I was only a little boy when my father and mother started taking me clamming. We all went, even the youngest. I remember being out there when I was around seven. It's what we did when we went out on a boat on the Great South Bay. The bay is some forty-five miles long, a few miles wide, separated from the Atlantic Ocean by a thin strip called Fire Island. It's full of smaller islands and marshes and shallows. It is tidal. It's full of clams, hard clams in different sizes. Some spots are more productive than others. It's really a beautiful place, the great south bay. We spent a lot of time there as kids with the family. I remember that we'd all get on the boat and head out past the Cross Bay channel into the islands, inlets, and shallows where there was a good ocean flush. My dad would throw an anchor over and command, "Everybody get out of the boat and get clamming." He didn't care how cold the water was, but I sure did.

The clams are categorized into four sizes. The categories are little necks, top necks, cherry stones, and chowders. We would catch mostly the larger ones. But there would always be a couple of little necks in half a pail of clams. They like a muddy bottom, a couple inches of mud with sand on top. It felt kind of nice on your feet.

You have to be a little careful because that mud can get up to your knees, deep. There were also crabs to look out for. They would bite your toes. Often you couldn't see them until they nipped your toes.

The best time to clam depended on the tide. Low tide was best when the water was only up to your knees. By high tide, it was up to your chest, and you'd have to go under the water to pull the clam out of the bottom. I never grew tired of going clamming with my family. I like doing it even until this day.

There's a special feel when you step on one — you know it's a clam. They are hard and have a ridge just sticking a hair above the surface. It sends off an alarm, "Got one!" and you know it. Sometimes, you'd have to dig the big chowders out of the mud and sand with your fingers. They would jam in there tight, and it took work to remove them. All this was a pleasant experience. When I was a boy, my family all liked to eat clams, except me.

I would try every season to eat one. Nope. I was a fussy eater. The way they looked — slimy. I just couldn't get past that. I kept trying. I wanted so badly to like clams. I would try the smallest ones. Everybody else was sloping them down. I tried them with cocktail sauce thinking that would help. It didn't.

I think when I got past how they looked and concentrated on the taste, I finally came to really like them. That was in my early twenties. I could taste the sweetness in them. It was unexpected in something that looked so gross and slimy.

I still love raw clams, but you have to get them home and on ice and eat them within three days or the sweetness goes away. Clamming and eating clams, they go together. You can't buy that at the grocery store.

MORNING WALK

I've been walking lately instead of going to the gym. It's really a good workout. I break a good sweat. It's been a month or so, three times a week. I walk up Redwine Plantation Drive to Happy Valley Circle. It's a two-mile walk. I walk on the side without a sidewalk down towards the clubhouse, and I take the sidewalk side back. I was rained out a couple of days this week. It's been in the 90s but in the morning only in the 70s. You want to go in the mornings when it's nice outside.

Sometimes it's hard to get going and you make excuses in your mind, but I'm starting to like the walks. So today, I started out walking on a stretch of moss. It's very nice, like walking on a carpet. There's quite a stretch of moss on the walk. I notice how pretty it looks, deep yellow and green. More brilliant than I remember. I also notice small white mushrooms coming up with what looks like tiny white buildings on top of them. I see the Spanish moss coming up out of the ground and small plant shoots.

I'm looking down as I go, and I see a cicada, and it's white. I thought it might be something else, but I got down on my knees to get a closer look. It looks like a cicada. I grab its wings, and it starts making a cicada sound. I don't remember them doing that in the past.

Usually they just vibrate their wings. I thought maybe I had woken him up. He was startled.

I think how everything's so green because of the rain we had. God uses rain to nourish the earth. You can see that this morning. It's very encouraging to me to see that today. I'm walking back on the sidewalk and there are these small acorns everywhere. They are only about a quarter of an inch big.

I'm heading up further and notice that they've cleaned the bridge on Island Cove, cut back all the trees and bushes. I took a little tour to go look. The creek runs under there, maybe I can see some fish. I'm looking up the creek and there's a beaver dam. It looks nice. I notice something I've seen before there — relief vents where water comes through the dam. The beavers put them in there to stabilize the dam. I've seen it often enough that I now believe it's intentional and part of the way beavers construct their dams.

I head home after a beautiful trip.

WINDOWSILLS

There are jobs around the house that have to be done. If you don't see them all the time, they can skip your mind. Well, I had a job like that, a windowsill in the upstairs, unfinished part of the house. It's just insulated, heated and air conditioned. The windowsill which is made of pressboard and covered in plastic was coming apart. It was so deteriorated it was in two pieces, and water was leaking into the house. It was in bad shape when I bought the house, but it was out-of-sight and out-of-mind.

I thought I might have to get a new window, but I was looking online and saw that I could just get a new windowsill. It looked pretty easy to do. The website said they had some in stock at Lowes. They had a seven-foot-piece of sill and a nose piece. I didn't need one that long, but they didn't have anything shorter, so I bought it. It fit in the cab of the truck right through the sliding back window. I was surprised. It looked like it was made for that. It made me like my new truck a little more. I got some caulking, too.

I got back home and cut out the rotten sill and transposed the lengths of the old sill to the new one. It went on nicely. I glued the nose piece on with PVC glue. It looked like a new window. I was very happy, and I had a leftover piece for another window.

Jacki was looking at a window over the garage, and that sill was deteriorated, too. There's a big unfinished room over the garage. I'm looking at it, and I agree that it needs a new sill. However, I saw a lot of ants on the window. I wondered what they were doing up there. I sprayed some ant killer on the sill and below and decided to replace the sill another day.

A couple days later, I started cutting the sill out. It came out good. I cut the new one from the leftover piece, and I had it installed in less than an hour. I'm screwing the screen holding the bolt into the sill and the screw falls out of the window. There's a gutter right there about four feet down and two feet out. I can't see the screw, but I can't see the whole width of the gutter. I don't have another screw for the latch. The extension ladder is right on the side of the garage. I got the ladder and put it up on the garage. I only have to extend it up a few rungs to reach the gutter. I climb up and look in the gutter. It's not there. I can't believe it.

I notice the bottom of the J channel is lower than the bottom of the siding. I decided to fix that while I have the ladder here. I start pulling the siding out of the J channel and there's a seam in the siding, and I'm pulling it out and bending it away from the house so I can see why it's hanging down. I notice there's orange-brown water in the J channel. I see a graying brown piece of something in the J channel. I reach over to grab it, and it jumps out of the J channel and lands in the gutter. It hops down the gutter to the end and makes a right turn, and it's gone. I'm surprised, very surprised. Did I see a toad behind the siding on the second story of my house? Yes. Yes, I did.

Why is it up here? And why do I have an estuary on the second story of my house for toads? Pretty cool.

SCALLOPS

Scallops have a pretty and attractive shell with a fan shape. I remember seeing their shells around the bottom of the bay while we were out clamming or when we were close to the beaches. We'd pick them up. I brought many home. I only remember seeing one live one. My father got one when we were clamming. I remember my mom would make scallops for dinner once in a while. I wasn't a real fan, but I could eat them. Mom would cook them in bacon fat.

My first real scallop encounter was in Southold in the late eighties. My real estate agent John Deritter would go out with his dad and cousin in Narrow River on Long Beach Bay. It was an area of Orient, New York. There was a season for scallops. I was more of a spectator on my trip with the Deritters. John was off the boat with a mask and snorkel. He got a bunch, a couple of bushels. We went to his dad's house after and opened them — Peconic Bay Scallops. I started to like them raw. They are a little hard to open. One half of the shell is larger than the other half. You hold the bigger part in the hand facing down, and you stick a knife through the hinge side. It takes a lot of practice to be good at it. I never really got good at it. I could open them, but it was a little bit of an ordeal.

There were quite a few shucking shacks when I first moved to Southold. I remember the season opened October first in the late 1980s when I first went scalloping with the Deritters. In the 90s, it changed to November first. It was much nicer when the season opened in early October. When November first was opening day, it could get quite cold. I can tell that the photo I have must have been in November when Jacki and I took her mom, Grandma Fay, because we are wearing heavy jackets and hats. That trip started because of all the talk about scallops with Grandma Fay. She loved the idea of getting fresh free seafood. In Amityville she was always crabbing at the dock at the foot of Ocean Avenue. She was very successful at catching crabs.

The day we took Grandma Fay to hunt for New York State's tastiest scallop, The Peconic Bay Scallop, started out cold and breezy. Not my kind of day to be on the water. We headed out to Orient to put in our 14-foot aluminum boat on Narrow River Road. It's really Grandma Fay's boat, but that's another story. It had a red and white 1959 18-horsepower Johnson Motor. So, we get out there.

I can't see the bottom. It's cold. It's breezy. It's not going to be a good day. I would have called it off, but Grandma Fay was determined. I didn't say anything, so we're out there and can't see a thing through the water.

There's no way to see the scallops and know where and how to scoop with the crab nets. Grandma Fay starts randomly and blindly going over the bottom with her net. I'm thinking, "Well, we will just have to let her wear herself out trying." But low and behold, she gets one. And another. And then Jacki starts getting some. I start trying, too, and I get some. I think we ended the trip with the better part of a bushel of Peconic Bay Scallops.

Then I had to go home and try to open them up.

WHAT I DO EVERYDAY

I was asked by a friend at church what I do every day. That's a pretty big question. I'm not sure I can answer it. Usually that question would be, "What do you do for a living." Since I do very little to make a living, I think one thing I do is practice awareness about what's going on around me. My focus has shifted from making a living. My focus has shifted from work to life: doing things around the house, taking care of the lawn, fixing things, gardening, putting down chips, trimming bushes, and the like. But I think the real joy is noticing things that are happening around me. I'm going to mention a few of these things.

This week I was on my morning walk and returning back almost to my street. A young black lab walking with his owner passed by. I'd met the owner once before when he was out back with one of his sons. As I walked over to greet him, the dog was hesitant, so I waited for it to come over, reached down to pet her, and she became my best friend. As she turned the corner to move away, walking right alongside her master, I could not but notice how happy that dog was. Her tail was wagging in a way that I knew was happy — in circles. Her body was clumping along, not pulling or straining, but just happy to be out for a walk. I've thought this week how I could describe it better, but I don't have different words. She was just one happy little dog.

My next tale this week is about a small boy next door, three years old, who loves to talk. He was walking in the backyard after his cat. He was calling him in that little voice, and the cat heard him and was wagging his tail. You could tell that they were pals. I was working in the garage, so I started walking over to him. His dad came over and was talking to his son, so I asked his Dad how old he was. His dad said, "Tell Mr. Baxter how old you are." He tried to get three fingers together. He had three different ways and was trying hard. His dad was helping him, but three fingers ticking up—not yet.

We have a young lady neighbor, a mom, who needed a heart transplant and was waiting for a heart donor. Finally, a donor was located. Andrea had to go to Nashville for a few months, maybe as long as five months. She has a cat, Binky, a friendly cat that she loves. Binky comes by often for a visit. Binky also keeps the chipmunk population in check. She likes to sleep in a chair on our front porch. Binky was there the other day laying in the chair. I went out, and I was rubbing and petting Binky. She liked it. Our community has a Facebook page that maintains updates for and about Andrea, so I posted about my visit with Binky. Andrea wrote back the nicest thank you that I have ever received: *Mr. Mark, Happy Tears over here. Thank you so much for loving on her. We miss her so much. We are blessed to have you as such an amazing neighbor. God bless you!*

I also trimmed the weeds out of the street with a weed eater this week. I finally learned how to tap the line box and have the line extend. After all these years, such a victory, this side of glory!

One more thing, we have a new Publix on Hwy 29. At lunch time, I drove over and got some potato soup. I parked out back of the store and ate the soup. It was good. After lunch, I got out of the truck and walked to Williams Lake. I'd been wanting to go there and fish for a while, but I wasn't sure how I was going to do that. The last time I was here, it looked fishy but a little shallow.

So today I was going to have another look. It's pretty far into the woods. The last time, I got lost and I had to walk out the 29 following the noise from the highway. This time, I used the GPS on my phone. There's not one path that goes to the lake. On my way in, it's pretty thick. I'm pushing through. I see on the ground what looks like a lemon. I'm wondering how that got there. Who dropped it? I start looking up, and I see one hanging there. I take my phone out and use the plant app that I have to discover that it's a purple passion fruit, a

Maypop. I take one with me — maybe I'll try to eat and save the seeds to grow at home.

One more and I'm done. I went to one of my favorite fishponds full of lily pads and beavers and picked up two bags of bottles and cans that people leave there.

These are some of the things I do every day besides reading through the New Testament slowly, one chapter a day.

.

SPLITTING WOOD FOR MY DAD

I think I started splitting wood when I was twelve
years old. My father loved burning wood in his fireplace.
He had a Heatalator on the fireplace, which is a metal box
with four air vents on it, two on each side, one high and
one low, both sides. It also had a screen and andirons that
you laid the logs on. Some years later, he got a brass trim
glass door with cast iron grates to help burn a longer fire.
He had a set of fireplace tools which he used a lot. As I'm
thinking back, he really did love burning wood. The
second extension he built on the house had a wood door
from the outside so he could store wood between the two
closets in the little room and he wouldn't have to go
outside to add wood to the fire. He also built a garage, the
third extension. It had a room off the back with a lower
roof that he stored split wood in to dry. He also had a bin
built into it to store kindling. He really had a great setup
for burning wood in the fireplace. He kept the brass
trimmed fireplace door shining and the glass doors clean.
He would tell me many times about the ashes building up
under the grate. It would disfigure the cast iron if the ashes
built up to the bottom. He had his grate the whole time he
used the fireplace. Also, he said that you had to have hot
fires to keep creosote from building up on the chimney

liner. He said to never use wet wood. From time to time, you would hear of a chimney fire in town that the fire department was called out on. I remember at times, Dad had it so hot in the living room, you couldn't sit in there with him. I thought he was going to catch the living room on fire.

Later in life, after many different stoves and places I'd lived, I understood that you just can't get warm in the winter unless you have that hot heat from a wood fire. It warms you to the bones. I really can't remember the first stack of wood I split, or how many piles I split, but it was quite a lot, and I got good at it. I was pretty fast at it. My dad had an ax, a couple of wedges, and a 3-pound lump hammer to bang wedges into the wood. I remember one of the new tools that came around was a splitting maul. We finally got one when I was around 14. I would split the wood on the garage apron. There are still chips in the apron. My father got a piece of three-quarter inch plywood to put down and protect the apron.

I learned a lot about different types of wood — which ones split the easiest, which ones were the hardest. Wild cherry was the toughest. I'd have two wedges and two axes all the way in and then I'd try to pull it apart with my hands and feet. I think this wood splitting made me a better wrestler in high school. There were times that I complained, but it was my job, and my father really enjoyed burning firewood.

As I grew and got my own house, set up my own wood stoves, and then built my own house with two fireplaces, and a wood potbelly stove in the basement — it all started here with splitting wood for my dad, even when I didn't want to.

MRS. D'ANDREA, MY FAVORITE TEACHER

I haven't thought of my favorite teacher or teachers in probably fifty years, but we have all had them. My story starts at Powell's Funeral Home on Broadway in Amityville, some six years ago. The funeral was for a woman named Stevens, an accountant at the Jim Wandel Company, who did my taxes for years. Her father and my father were best friends as kids. They belonged to the same gang, The Green Onion Gang. The boys had to swim from end to end of Avon Lake to belong. I was there paying my respects.

There was an elderly man there in his 90s. He came over to me, and I introduced myself, and he told me he was Mr. D'Andrea. "Oh," I said, "was your wife Mrs. D'Andrea, my school teacher?" He said she was and told me about her long tenure as a schoolteacher in Amityville. He wondered if her work had any real value. I almost started to cry. I was sniffling, choking up. I was thinking about Mrs. D'Andrea. I haven't thought about her in years. He said goodbye, and I was off to Southold.

I thought to myself, I have to write him a note and tell him how much I loved Mrs. D'Andrea, and that she was the best teacher I ever had. I remember calling my sisters to get his address. He lives in Snug Harbor. I got the address; I sat down at my desk and started to scribble down some things. Four lines was all I could come up with. I tried again, and again, and again. I could not write a letter to Mr. Andrea and tell him, "Yes! Mrs. D'Andrea's teaching career was very valuable. Especially to me."

I loved Mrs. D'Andrea, as much as a nine-year-old can. She was my favorite teacher that I've ever had. She had an impact on Mark Baxter. Sometimes our emotions and feelings outlast our memories. I still have the emotions, and for that I'm grateful.

At the time, behind my desk, I could not put these thoughts into words. Some years later, my daughter Katherine gave me a book about writing things about my life's history. So I thought maybe I could learn how, and I signed up at the University of West Georgia, to see if maybe I could write a few of my memories.

I'm in my second year and my professor, Mrs. Jackson, has been meeting with me for a good part of the year on Tuesdays and Thursdays. I've made much progress in my writing. I was doubtful that I would be able to write, but we have a website, and I have written sixty stories in the Writing Center at UWG. It has brought back many memories that I thought were gone. Meeting Mr. D 'Andrea in the funeral was a catalyst to do this to express my love for a fourth-grade teacher, Mrs. D'Andrea. For that, I am thankful. Thank you.

This was six years in the coming. I finally got to write my letter to Mrs. D'Andrea.

MILITARY SERVICE

Sept 1970-June 1973

It was a heck of a journey. I learned a lot. One of the big things I learned how to do was take care of myself. It wasn't easy. But I say it saved my life. I was headed the wrong way back home, and I got a glimpse of the right way. It was the discipline that I needed.

Growing up I heard so much about the military from my dad. He told me so many stories – many times the same ones. He joined after the Japanese bombed Pearl Harbor. He said the line at the recruitment center stretched around the corner with men like him ready to sign up. He was an officer. He went to OCS in Fort Benning, Georgia. He was in the 101st Cavalry in Maine. He was GUNG HO! He ended up going to the Pacific. He supplied the troops as they moved up the island chain. My father loved our country. He thought it was the greatest country in the world, as I do.

My service enlistment started in Bay Shore, New York. They had a program that helped get you some rank right out of basic training, E4 Specialist, if you had skills in plumping, electrical, or carpentry. So, I went to take a test at Fort Hamilton in Brooklyn, and I passed. I signed up for three years. Basic training was at Fort Dix, New Jersey.

It was tough. All the yelling, getting up early, making beds, cleaning the barracks. I could sleep standing up. That's how tired I was.

My next duty station was Fort Leonard Wood, Missouri. It was beautiful country, full of rivers. I was in Headquarters Company. I didn't do a whole lot. I went to the motor pool most mornings. A lot of the talk was about Vietnam and what went on there. Many of the men had just returned.

I loved all the stories and after some time speaking with them, I thought, I have to go there. I had a friend from California, Frank Buckner. He said he knew someone in the orders department on base. He said he could get me orders to go to Vietnam. I said, great! Two weeks later, I had orders for Vietnam.

I got to go home for a few weeks, then off to Vietnam. It was the longest plane trip I've even taken: New York to Seattle to Hawaii to Cameron Bay in Vietnam. I stayed overnight in Cameron Bay at the south end of Vietnam. My orders were for Danang. I remember looking at the map to figure out where that was. It was all the way north. When I saw that, I thought I was going to be on the front line right at the North Vietnamese border. It sure seemed close.

We boarded a C15A cargo plane up the aft ramp where they load the equipment and supplies. I walked in and sat on a canvas seat that folded down from the side of the plane. There were just three or four of us headed to Danang that day. An hour or so later, we landed in Danang on the South China Sea. When they came to get me and drive me through Danang, I couldn't get over how many fenced in bases there were. They were everywhere and BIG.

I was only in my first camp for a couple of weeks before racial tensions within the camp erupted. They broke up the whole company and moved us around. I didn't even know what it was about. The next camp was Camp Warlong right on the South China Sea. The first camp wasn't on the water, but this one was. We weren't allowed to have guns on base. You didn't really need them unless you were on guard duty, which I was quite often.

A lot of things happened. A typhoon came through which kept us busy for a while repairing the damage. Bob Hope came to visit. Bob Hope was way better than I thought he'd be. There must have been five or six hundred soldiers in the stadium, and they really loved him. When he swung his golf club on stage, the whole place went crazy.

There are a lot of stories about things that happened here. This is probably not the most worthy one, but it's the one that got me thinking about my trip to Vietnam.

I was listening to some of the guys talk about the ARVN (Army of the Republic of Vietnam) base that they were working on. It was some distance away, but they were doing major work, building a kitchen, mess hall, bathrooms, and more. They said they had a chef who was cooking some amazing food out there.

The stories kept coming. So, I said, maybe I could go out there with them and eat some of that chef's food. I think they needed some help with plumbing, so I got to go out there. There were two plumbers already on the job, and they didn't want me messing up their work, so the NCO in charge put me on installing a dechlorinizer injector, not a big deal. I didn't care. I didn't come out here to do some plumbing. I came out here for lunch.

Lunch came and I was asking around— What are we having for lunch?

Hot dogs.

Hot dogs?

It was Friday, and they always had hot dogs on Friday. I thought, maybe they have something else. An extra side dish? Something special?

I remember walking into the mess hall and seeing what looked like a huge pan of boiled hot dogs. Hot dogs, it is.

Just thinking about it, I can almost taste them. It almost makes me cry.

The BEST hotdogs I've EVER had.

CHRISTMAS CARDS WITH MOM

This story happened sometime back at Mom's house at Christmas time. The homestead — six kids were brought up there, 1200 square foot house. My mom was a good mom. She did so much for her kids. Cleaned all our clothes, made the beds, cleaned the house, and put up with me and all the other kids, and was a great cook. I couldn't really eat food cooked by someone else. I miss her very much.

This story is about Christmas time. I was over to visit Mom and noticed that she had not made out her Christmas card that year. The house was always decorated with Christmas cards every year. They were around the mantel, both sides, and around the door frames, sometimes around the shelves that Dad built.

My parents really outdid themselves for Christmas. The tree, the presents, it was a special time for the family in the Baxter house.

My mom was having medical issues and was not going to make out Christmas cards that year. I encouraged her to, and I would fill them out. She had the cards, so we set out to do that job. I had fun doing that with my mom even though my handwriting leaves a lot to be deserved. She had the addresses and papers with names on them that she would take out every Christmas. We made out the cards.

There weren't as many as I remembered. But many people Mom knew were gone. It was fun, and Mom was pleased. We kind of got in the Christmas spirit. So, I was pleased, too. It was getting late and I had to drive to Southold, about an hour away. It was a special time with my mom many years ago, as I reflect on it now.

I didn't know it would be the last time I would see my mom alive. She had chest pains three days later, and on the ride to the hospital, she passed away. I remember that mom wanted to have ice cream after we finished the cards that night. I said it was late and I had to go. I regret not having ice cream that night with my mom, but I also rejoice that I had that time with her. It was a special time. I will always remember it.

You cannot do a kindness too soon, for you never know when it will be too late.

THE SAME CAST

One evening after work, I drove my van across a vacant, unplanted, farm field in Riverhead, NY, going uphill toward the elevated tree line to another dirt road that wound its way around a secret pond — secret to me. It backs up to the Long Island Sound. I love to look back over the fallow farm field and toward the old farm house. I wish I had taken a couple of photos of the scene. I would always take a moment to look out over the field. I still wonder why I liked it so much.

There is a small spot right by the pond where I could squeeze the van into park. Trees and underbrush surround the pond. You can wader the whole 5-acre pond, all the way around — which I do, when I go. It's one of my favorite places to be. I don my waders over my work clothes and get my fishing pole, and fill the little storage pouch at the top of my waders with one bag of Gary Yamamoto worms. I fish with a few hooks, number three offset. It takes about an hour to wader all the way around, depending on how many fish I catch. I always go to the east, the right, when I fish there.

About halfway around the pond, I make a cast and love the way the stick bait raises a high arch in the air. It reminds me of a cast I made here some years back. It seemed it just suspended itself while this thought came into my mind. It was the same cast, in the same place, on the same pond that I had made years earlier. And that time I caught a five-pound largemouth bass which is a trophy fish up north.

As the bait hits the water, I'm smiling and lost at the thought of that experience. I'm startled and brought back to the present by my pole bent in half with a big bass in excess of five pounds—a dream startled by another dream.

Could fishing get any better? I let the fish go and finished the loop. I wish I had a picture.

PLAYALINDA BEACH

Playa Linda Beach is located on Florida's East
Coast in the Cape Canaveral National Seashore in
Titusville. In Spanish, the name means "Pretty Beach," and
it truly is. It was a long drive coming east over the national
seashore over bridges and wetlands. Playa Linda is the
longest beach in the state of Florida with 24 miles
stretching north and south. It was interesting to see the
campers camping right on the road where there was room
to park with their chairs and canopies out.

It was in the high seventies, low eighties in Florida
that day, and I thought they were probably escaping the
cold up north. It was snowing in New Jersey. I knew that
because I had gotten a text from Katherine that the kids
were making a snowman. We came to the gate of Ocean
Beaches and pulled into the number three parking area. I
saw a high bluff going all the way down one side of the
parking lot with stairs and platforms and a boardwalk. I
could hear the waves crashing on the beach. We all got out
of the car and headed over.

We walked down to the beach. Looking both
ways, I could see nothing but water and beach, blue as the
Caribbean, as far as the eye could see. The smell of the
ocean brought back a lot of memories of going to the

ocean beaches up in New York. The first look always stuns and impresses me. I'm glad I'm there. I had to test out and feel the sand and water. I took off my shoes and rolled my pants up, and me and Jacki and Sean headed to the water.

The sand felt great on my feet. Soon the soft sand got hard just before we got to the water. As we approached, I was a little apprehensive about how cold the water would be. It was cold but not too cold — just right. I was enjoying the waves coming in and breaking — the white colors, the blue colors, the smell, the view down the beach, the crispness of the salt water on my legs. I didn't think it would be this enjoyable, but it was.

The other beach goers were starting to pack up. There was a magic in the air like remembrance — like something that we will all remember and like something that I was remembering. With tears in my eyes. I said out loud in a low voice, "I don't deserve this." I surprised myself by saying that.

I too am going home soon. No more tears, no more sorrow, but joy forever more. Hope of Heaven — a little foretaste of that this afternoon.

SECRET POND

One of my favorite spots to fish, and to be, is on the Long Island Sound in Riverhead, New York. It's about six acres and higher than the North Road which Hallicksville is on. The pond used to provide irrigation for a farm enterprise from 1810 into the mid-20th century. I like to tell the story about my first trip up there with my two sons, Tom and Sean, my fishing buddies.

We located this pond on a map of the North Fork. We've found several ponds this way. I love the mystery and fun of going to a new pond—a new fishing spot. Over the years there have been many. It starts out as it always does in a van with a couple of fishing poles and a dream of that big bass and off we go with both sons sharing the front bucket seat. When they were small they fit just fine in that bucket seat.

We head out on the North Road west towards Riverhead. There is a gate and fencing on the west end of the property and to the side of the gate an old road runs alongside the overgrown fence. We take the dirt road all the way to the back of the property beyond the farm fields. We start making our way east toward Secret Pond. There were some dilapidated cabins and wooden structures. I found out later that it was a boy scout camp many years prior. The Long Island Sound is just a few hundred feet beyond the structures. It's close enough that if you listened you could hear the water. There are some dirt roads going east winding in and through the woods as we worked our way toward the Secret Pond. We are getting further away from the van following the winding trails by instinct.

I'm getting excited. We are all searching — looking for a glimpse of that new pond. Who will be the first one there, and who will make the first cast? I'm pretty sure we can't miss it. We just keep going forward. There's no road now. We keep going through the thick woods. Finally, we get a glimpse through the underbrush — water. We push through the thorny underbrush. We come into the pond on the north side. There's a little sandy spot of shoreline — not much to cast from. Tom was the first one ready to cast. Sean was still looking for another spot. Tom threw out a jointed Rapala. His first cast and he has one on. It's a yellow perch, the biggest one I ever saw and the biggest one since. It was a very good beginning to a new pond. Although we still call it Secret Pond, its location is no longer a secret to us. This was the beginning of a long relationship with Secret Pond.

A FISH STORY

This story starts on a summer evening — a beautiful evening— on Great Pond. Just me and Tom on Grandma Fay's boat. I'm very partial to nice weather to go out fishing or wading. I've called myself a "fair weather sailor." It doesn't always work out that way. This evening it did.

We started on the north side of Great Pond and worked our way east because we fish her so much there are spots that we know the bass like, and there are cattails along the shoreline that the fish like to lay in. We have stories for fish caught all along the way.

When Sean is with us, there's a little fighting over who gets to cast in those spots. Well tonight wasn't one of those nights. Tom was in the front of the boat and had the first cast in all the best spots.

Even so, we could not get a hookup — not that we weren't trying. Could have been because it was summer and the fish had moved offshore, out of the warm water.

Over the years, I've gotten more joy from just being out here with my sons: Catching fish is not the only reason to be here. But I felt Tom's disappointment. I really wanted to put him on to some fish. I was the pilot that night. We were halfway around the pond, and we were coming up to the big boulder. I always fish that area when wading. Sometimes the pond gives up fish there, a deep area between the boulder and the cattails at the shoreline.

With a lot of confidence, I told Tom there's a big one in that spot between the rock and the weed line. Tom didn't believe me, but I was confident and repeated, "Tom, cast over there." Tom still didn't believe me, so I told him that I was going to cast over there.

I cast over there.

I immediately had a big one on. I wasn't sure how big, but it turns out to be the biggest bass that I've ever caught. It weighed seven pounds and eight ounces. To this day, it is still the biggest.

How did I know that?

LAUREL LAKE

Just thinking about Laurel Lake puts a smile on my face. It's a thirty-acre lake, forty-five feet deep, and very good for swimming. There are few houses on it. There was a Girl Scout camp there years ago. There is still a remnant of a walkway going out on the east end of the lake. It gets deep quickly. There's bass, perch, pickerel, and bluegill in the lake. In fact, the New York state record bluegill came from here.

Laurel Lake is the only lake on the North Fork that the state stocks trout in. The access is off the main road down behind a ballfield off a dirt and gravel road. Then there's a hundred-yard path, a dirt walkway, that leads to the lake. Beautiful rhododendrons cover the sides of the path which is pretty steep. The access along the water is limited especially in Springtime when the water is higher. I like coming here in the summertime when it is hot out, especially in the afternoon after work to get a swim in cool lake water and maybe catch a few fish. I would often walk in the shallows of the lake with no shoes. This leads to one story I have been thinking about of late. This is one of many stories from Laurel Lake.

One summer afternoon I was coming home from a job, it was hot out, and I thought I would go for a swim.

As usual I brought a fishing pole and a red Gary Yamamoto worm with me. I really was more interested in a swim than fishing that day, but why not do both. The water is always clear with a sandy bottom. This afternoon, I'm fishing and swimming in the west end of the lake. I walk out into the water to chest height and come back toward shore to my waist. I caught one before I got to the corner where there is a small dock. You can't see a house there at all because there's woods around it. Beyond the dock there's really no access to the water because of cattails and lily pads. I'm almost to the corner casting out in front of the dock when I get a fish on but lose my bait, my Gary Yamamoto worm.

Well, I guess I'm going home, I think. I look around the dock hoping maybe there's something I can use, and low and behold, there's a red Gary Yamamoto worm hanging from the handrail from a piece of monofilament. The only thing there. I decided if it was mine, I would share it with another fisherman. So, I reached up, took it off the hook, put it on my hook, and gave it a good heave. It hits water. I'm waiting and enjoying being here in this beautiful place when the line starts moving off. I set the hook, and I fought in a five-pound largemouth bass.

I let the bass go and let's say I put the red Gary Yamamoto worm back on the hook hanging from the dock—for the next guy. Truth is, I don't remember anything else after catching that five-pound bass.

I love that story.

OPENING DAY

The weather was right — the temperature was perfect. The spring had sprung. The trees had started to leaf out —it's one of my favorite seasons. Life punching out everywhere. The colors of new leaves: the greens, the yellows, and the reds, and the browns. Truly glorious to the smallest and the biggest — it's happening all around us.

The same thing is happening to me. I have to go trout fishing. I usually have to take a drive to get there. The cool morning, no wind and life sprouting out all around me. A good start of the day. I've got my waders, my fish bag, filled with stuff. I head off to two local ponds — no trout there but such a beautiful spring morning, and I get to wear my waders and take in this beautiful morning.

I arrive at the spot, and there's no one there. Good start. Using a small stick bait from Walmart, I head off through the woods with waders over my shoulder and head towards the water. It's a short walk down to the ponds. I'm standing on the edge of the pond looking across the pond at the trees and water line. The trees glisten; the pond glistens. No wind — just a nice spot to be for opening day.

I make a dozen casts. Nothing. I decided to take out my garbage bag and pick up some trash which is something I like to do. And while I'm doing that, I notice a very interesting tree stump that a beaver cut down, but it was the way it was chiseled that struck me. It had rectangular chisel marks almost like he was chiseling out a door lock. I might have to go back and cut that away to bring it home. There, also, alongside it, I see a small log grounded in the water. It has no bark, but I can tell that a beaver had chiseled it down. I may have to go get that one, too. I might start a collection.

I finish picking up stuff and grab my pole and waders and hike down to a spot where I wanted to make a few stick casts. There's a spot there — the first time I fished there I had a big one on.

I was walking between the two ponds along the berm, and I glimpsed a small sandy path in the water where the beaver travels. I knew this because my father had explained it to me a lifetime ago — I think I was ten. That was the password and pin to start me thinking about so many outdoor experiences. It was like it set off a tape — I couldn't stop it, nor did I want to:

Trapping muskrats and mice in Amityville

Fishing Avon lake when my wife was pregnant

Clamming in the Great South Bay

Things done or talked about with my father that
led to trips with my own boys, so many trips
        My own son showing me his fishing spots in
Florida, telling me his stories
        All God's mercies and blessings to me
        This life fitted together
        And I thought I was going fishing on opening day.

MCKAY POND

McKay Pond is an eight-acre pond on River Road
and Grumman Boulevard in Calverton. Over the years
fishing in this area, I passed it all the time. It was fenced in
on the Grumman property. Grumman is a big military jet
airplane builder and tester for the Navy. The F-14 Tomcat,
A-6 Intruder, E-2 Hawkeye, E-6B Prowler and other
aircraft are built and tested there. The runway is two miles
long, and there are armed gates in and out. Lots of Dads
when I was a kid worked out there. They tested the Lunar
module there, too. This was a pretty locked up place. It
reminded me of a military base, so I never thought that I'd
get to fish there.

Things changed, and Grumman wanted to move
and did. The property was in transition. The feds were
going to give it to the town of Riverhead. In this
transitional time, a gate on the east end of the pond was
open. There was my opportunity to drive in and park by
the pond to try a new spot. It really never looked that fishy
— no lily pads, some cattails, and a few trees and some
bushes growing on the side. I was just kind of curious how
it would be. Honestly, I didn't think it would be a good
fishing spot, but there's something about trying a new
pond. I just had to do it.

I never saw anybody fishing there, but this was my chance. Hopefully nobody would chase me, and there would be some fish in the pond. I parked on the grass and got out, fishing pole and Gary Yamamoto worm in hand. There's always some excitement when you go into a new spot. You don't know if it's going to be fishy, big fish, lots of fish, some fish, what you're going to see, or if you'll get chased off or in trouble.

First cast, I had a fish on. Second cast, had a fish on. Third cast, had a fish on. All bass, about two pounds. I soon realized that I was using up worms and switched to a floating Rapla stick bait. At every cast going around the pond, I had a fish on. I lost count at thirty. My arm was hurting. There's something about fishing — you just can't stop catching fish. I don't understand that. You just can't stop when the fish are hitting and every cast comes back with one on. This ain't fishing; this is catching.

I've heard that from other fishing people. One fellow told me he was fishing in the ocean with some of his friends on a boat. And they were catching one fish after another, and they were keeping them. He thought he was going to sink his boat with fish because they couldn't stop catching. He had to take off with the boat to stop it, because they couldn't stop catching fish.

I look back at that experience, the pond that no one fished, glistening in broad daylight, and loaded with fish. I think I caught a hundred fish that day.

IN CELEBRATION OF WADERS

Having waders, in some ways, is like having a boat
— the entry level boat — the least expensive boat. Like
boats, they come in many different types, sizes, colors,
materials, price ranges, and they are transportable and self-
powered. Like some boats they are easy to take care of.
However, they have their limitations — depth of water,
roughness of water, temperature of water. I have used
them for a long time, over thirty years or so. Over the
years, I've purchased at least ten pairs.

They come in all kinds of different materials,
different prices, different configurations — boot foot,
stocking feet.

I really do like fishing in waders. There's
something about being right down in the water. You take
part in the adventure, especially in ponds. You see more
animal life, for sure. I enjoy looking for stuff, especially on
the bottom of the water. It's just more of an adventure. I
remember on my father's boat looking for things on the
bottom. I could spend hours and we did — looking for
eels or other wildlife like crabs and turtles.

I like the minimal-ness of waders. Not a lot of
other equipment besides a fishing pole, pack of worms,
and hooks that can be stored in the upper pockets of the

waders. It seems the animal kingdom thinks you're one of them when you're out there in waders. I know that muskrats think so. They will swim by within a foot, if you don't move.

You have to know the depth and bottom composition. Some experience and knowledge are needed but easily learned. Some caution in big and fast-moving water is necessary. Also new ponds, which I really like, take a little time to get to know. I usually just grab a stick long enough to test the depth and wader in at a spot where I can see the bottom. Once you know them, you can use waders more confidently. I don't like being in fast moving rivers with rocky bottoms. Situations like that require extra caution.

In most of the ponds I fish with waders, I have a route that I take. Some of them, you can walk all the way around. Some of them you can only walk part of the way around. It can be very enjoyable to fish in waders. For me, waist high or less is ideal. I like boot foot waders. They are simpler to put on and faster. My fishing trips usually last one hour or so. You can fish when it's pouring rain out with a rain jacket and waders.

As I'm writing this, I can't remember ever reading anything about the use of waders. As with a lot of things in life, you have to learn on the job through experience.

WHY I FISH

From time to time, I think about why I go fishing and what I like about it. This story starts at a plumbing job where I was disconnecting and installing a new sink. The man of the house is quite the fishing person and loves to talk about it. While I'm working, we talk about fishing. He has a lifetime of stories and pictures on his phone. He's telling me fishing stories and sharing pictures. I finished disconnecting the sink, and we are still talking about fishing. He's very knowledgeable, and I'm asking questions. It was an enjoyable chat.

I had to come back in two days to hookup the new sink and install the faucet and drain. We talked more about fishing baits, where to fish, and how to fish, and about our family. He inspired me to go fishing that night. I caught six small bass.

I got a call from him the next day — the hot and cold lines needed to be reversed. Of course, we kept talking about fishing. He had to open the garage, and I was looking at his fishing boat. He had eight bait casting poles with various different baits, lines, and reel retrieves. It was impressive. He was clearly a good and knowledgeable fisherman. We had another talk. He wanted to take me fishing. I declined and said another time.

That evening, I told Jacki, "I'm going fishing." I wanted to check out a pond that I fish regularly, and I wanted to try out some new baits I'd just bought from a young fellow in the neighborhood who started a business making different plastic baits.

I also wanted to check out the beavers and see how they were doing, so I headed down to the pond with four bags of fishing stuff in my pocket — it's a little crowded. I'm catching fish with the new baits and moving along the pond. It's a beautiful evening out. I'm starting to notice the grass and trees — how lush and thick everything was. I was enjoying being here in Georgia — yes, Georgia. I've been thinking about all the wildflowers I've been seeing along the highways, the yellow daisies and the Queen Anne's Lace with its distinct smell. Wonderful.

By now, I was at the end of the pond. There's a gate that goes to another field and goes up the creek to where the beaver ponds are. The first pond is small, about eighty feet around. I caught four bass there. I worked my way to the back beaver pond and noticed more mud on the beaver wall. I looked around the pond, and I saw a lot of small trees cut out along the water's edge. There was a dead tree in the middle with what looked like an owl's nest-sized hole three quarters of the way up with orange trumpet flowers starting to bloom around it. It was becoming more beautiful. I kept noticing things there. Could it be a beaver garden — For me or anyone else to stumble on and enjoy?

This is surely one of the reasons I go fishing. As John Muir put it, "and off into the forest I go to lose my mind and find my soul."

AVON LAKE

Avon Lake is a three-acre lake, long and fairly
narrow. The deepest spot is 18-feet deep. It's in Amityville,
NY. It has a road that goes all the way around it, trees
nearly all the way. It's fed by a stream that runs all year
around. It's off Avon Place and feeds into Amityville
Creek. We would see it every day walking to school
through Avon Place in the late 1950s and 1960s. The street
was lined with trees and older homes set back from the
road and facing the lake. A section of the northside had a
three-foot high wall because of the elevation with the top
of the wall on an angle. I'd always try to walk on that,
balancing as I made my way home from school.

The lake had carp and stocked trout, and now
they also have large-mouth bass. In my father's day, to
belong to his gang, boys had to swim from one end of the
lake to the other to earn membership. By the time we were
hanging around at the lake, it was too dirty to swim in.
Where the stream enters, the town erected a thirty-foot-
wide storm wall made of stone with a pipe that came
under the road. We'd sit up there, about six feet above the
water. That was the spot to fish from. The Amityville
Police Department, where my dad worked as Policeman
for twenty years, had an annual fishing contest and quite a

few people would come. I don't think I ever won anything or placed in the contest.

I remember one year I went, and they gave out ice cream. I think that's probably why I was there. Another year, an older guy, probably 18, was bottom fishing and wasn't paying much attention. His whole pole bent in half. He caught the biggest eel I have ever seen, even to this day. It was definitely the biggest fish caught that day, but they didn't have a category for eels. They gave him something anyway.

I really love Avon Lake. I spent a lot of time there as a kid. With many decades behind me and many fishing spots explored, I know now that as ponds go for fishing, Avon Lake is probably at the bottom of the list.

I had not been fishing there in a long time, but when Jacki was pregnant with Katherine, I would go there in the evenings. I don't really know why I went down there. I hadn't been fishing in a long time. I was doing business and busy setting up our life and coming family.

There were a few nights I went down there, and I'd get a carp on, but I'd lose them. Eventually, I was able to bring them a little closer to shore. Twenty years later, I learned from Steve that when you're fishing for carp, you have to put the pole down and let them take the bait and move off until they swallow. Before that they just hold the bait in their mouth.

I can't think about Avon Lake without remembering one special friend. Back in the 50's, we had a dog friend, a beagle named Cleo. She was fairly heavy. She wasn't our dog. She was Mr. Vitale's, but she loved the kids in the neighborhood. She would run behind our bikes when we went up to Reimer's Deli downtown about half-a-mile away on Route 110. One time, we were wandering around the train tracks with Cleo, and she crawled under the third rail. Her tail tipped that current, and she shot home squealing, fast as a bullet.

We would go fishing at Avon Lake, and Cleo would come with us. One day, we were fishing off the stone end, and Cleo was just walking around smelling the environment. She was just so happy to be with us. Richie Hilbert, our neighbor across the street, was casting off the stone wall spillway, and hooked Cleo in the back. We could not get the hook out. She would scream every time we pulled. We were just kids, and we didn't know how to remove the hook. She went home with that hook in her back, and nobody noticed.

A few weeks later, we were out with Cleo. We had all forgotten about the hook. But somebody noticed that the hook was still there. The flesh around it had begun to rot. I reached down, and the hook came right out. She was as good as new. She healed just fine and kept us company for a few more years. Eventually, Mr. Vitale offered Cleo to my family, but my mom didn't want a dog. I'm not sure what happened to Cleo after that, but she went on many adventures with us. Cleo was great company for us kids on Terry Avenue in Amityville. I could use a Cleo now. I'm still kind of mad at my mom for not letting us get a dog or keep Cleo.

I'm remembering all this because of one memory in particular that seems to infuse the fisherman I am now because of the boy I was then with Cleo at my side on the banks of Avon Lake. When trout season came it was time to stock the pond. The new trout would hang there where the stream entered the lake. As spring turned toward summer, they would go up the stream and hide out in the pipe under the road because it was cool and dark there in the protected tunnel that must have been about 100-feet long. I would go upstream to the other side of the road and drift worms on a small hook and a light unweighted line. As the worm worked its way under the road, boom, I'd feel that little shudder and tug, almost like rapping at a door, and I'd have one on. I still love fishing that way, with a light line and a worm, just drifting down to where the fish are. It's something I learned sixty years ago at Avon Lake, in the good company of a great dog.

DRIFT FISHING CENTERPIN WITH FRENCHIE

Centerpin fishing was relatively new to us in 2000 when we went to Pulaski, New York, to catch steelhead trout. Centerpin Fishing uses a longer rod somewhere between ten and thirteen feet and a free spinning reel with a large arbor. It looks like a fly reel. It has a free-spinning spool which really spins smoothly. It uses floats, (what I call bobbers, but they don't call them that) with split shots packed below the float depending on water condition, depth, and speed. It's a little hard to get used to. This specialty rod and reel was a tool to have for steelhead fishing.

I ended up getting a Sheffield rod, thirteen feet, four inches, and an Okuma Sheffield S 1002 reel in black. It was the most I'd spent on a rod and reel up to that time, around $350 to $400. I remember at the time, when I was picking out the rod, I picked out the one with the adjustable reel seat because I wanted to be able to adjust the reel seat to accommodate all the techniques involved in this type of fishing.

That was a mistake.

It was quite a change to fish a Centerpin setup. I remember we met this fellow at Fat Nancy's fishing store named Frenchie. I don't think he's French, but he does love to fish, probably to a fault. Frenchie was a good fisherman. He started a drift-boat fishing business, and he introduced us to Centerpin fishing. I think it was at Fat Nancy's that we first talked about it.

We hired Frenchie to take us on the Salmon River to fish with our new Centerpin reels and poles: me, Joe Russo, and my son Shawn. There are a few memorable things that stand out about fishing with Frenchie. For one, Frenchie loved fishing more than we did.

Frenchie wanted to meet up early, before dawn, at one of the boat ramps on the Salmon River. It was rainy, and we were a little late. We got lost finding the boat ramp. Frenchie liked being the first one on the river in the morning, and we were second.

We put in at the ramp and anchored up not too far from there, about a hundred yards down, if that. Shawn, Joe, and I were getting our Centerpins in the water. I remember sitting in the back with my pole and Frenchie telling me what I should be trying to do. There was a big rock down river about a hundred feet, and he said, "There's some steelhead there." My float is in the water and drifting down toward that rock.

He was speaking in a low, almost seductive, voice, saying "you're on the right track," "you're getting closer to the spot," "perfect drift," "a few more feet," "you're almost there," "looks perfect," "get ready", "you're on top of it."

He was way more excited than I was. With that low voice I was taken aback, as if he was calling the fish to me and me to the fish like a siren. That was our first stop on the river that morning.

There were fish caught on other spots that we anchored up to. We worked our way down to the old railroad crossing. I remember just after we passed under the railroad crossing, I had one on. I was fighting it. All of a sudden, my fancy adjustable-seat reel falls off into the river. I can see it down, seven feet. Because the reel has no stop, I lost my new reel. It was gone. I thought to myself that it was hard to be too disappointed. It was a beautiful spot on the river. I was with my son and my good friend Joe, and Frenchy.

I was probably still processing all of this, the loss of an expensive reel and the beauty of the trip, and Frenchie's strange and compelling way of getting inside my head and the fish's heads. But somehow, I can't even remember how, Frenchie got that reel off the bottom and back on my pole. Inconceivably, the fish was still on. And Frenchie got him to the boat, too. By that point, the fish hardly mattered; it had all been so exciting.

Some years later, we booked another trip with Frenchie. I asked him about the time he salvaged my reel from the bottom of the Salmon River. "I can't remember all my fish float trips," he said, "but I remember that."

ALMOST FALL FISHING TRIP

I got a text yesterday and the day before from my son Sean down in Florida with pictures of bass that he caught while fishing with a friend on his friend's bass boat. They fish a lot together. Beautiful, fishy looking water. I haven't been in a while. I've thought about it, but it's been very hot here in Georgia. I've been looking at the weather reports and temperatures at night are in the 60s, and it looks like the trend is cooler in the mornings. It could make for some good fishing.

I have to go to the bank today, but I stopped at a new coffee shop on the way to the spot. The office in front of the pond was closed, and it was very quiet. I reached into my fishing bag and grabbed the first bag on the top. It was Billet's Baits. I already had one on my pole. These are the baits made by my young neighbor in Lake Redwine. I grabbed my pole and walked through the woods down to the pond. The pond is three-quarters covered with duckweed. It could be good, I thought. The brush was a lot clearer along the water's edge than I remember. I noticed a couple of trees close to the water that beavers had chewed. It's just amazing how big the chips are when they are chiseling down a tree. I picked up a few — amazing.

I made a cast with the stick bait out between two clusters of lily pads. On the second cast, I get a hit — STRIKES really hard! I was surprised at how hard he hit. One fish on. I get him in, a twelve-inch fish but very feisty. I make another cast and another. Fourth cast. I pull it, and it seems like it's stuck on the bottom, but the line starts to move off. I pull and set the hook, and this big bass comes shooting out of the water. He's on! I let out a big howl! Fish on! Tom has a good howl when he catches a fish. It was similar to that.

The fish starts going sideways into the lily pads. I move up the pond, and I get him out. He jumps again. I let out another howl. His heading toward the other clump of lily pads. I move down the pond and he's coming in toward the shore. He jumps again. He's a big one! I let out another howl. There's a big log down by the shore below the water line. I don't want to, but I slide down the mud bank, and I'm standing in the water, I grab him by the lip and let out another howl. I got him! It's the biggest bass so far in Georgia. I wasn't expecting this. Thanks, Sean, for the fishing pictures motivating me to go. And thanks to the Good Lord for the adventure.

After I caught the big bass, I thought to myself I should go home, it won't get any better, but there was a lot going on down at the pond today:

The way the beavers cut down trees for the new roof in their house

The joy of seeing the silvery new roof

The wildflowers along the bank between the two ponds

The two-inch long bluegill another fish chased through the duck weed up to the shoreline

The call from Brit in the morning about a plumbing job on the very day I caught a bass with his son's bait

I thought the mulched dirt down at the shoreline would make good dirt for planting vegetables

All together it was a beautiful morning.

A FEW CASTS ON LONG ISLAND

Great Pond, Southold

Laurel Lake, Laurel

Wildwood Lake, South Hampton

Kaler's Pond, Center Moriches

Hashamomuck Pond, Mattituck

Sage Blvd Pond, Southold

Sill's Lane Pond, Southold

Marion Lake in East Marion

Narrow River, Long Beach Bay in Orient

Wolf Preserve Pond, Suffolk Co

Hommels Pond, Southold

Lily Pond in Suffolk Co

Goldsmith Inlet in Peconic

Orient Point in Orient

Lake Marratooka, Mattituck

Husing Pond, Mattituck

Manor Lane Pond, Jamesport

Hallock Pond, Riverhead

Penny Pond, Hubbard County Park

Bellows Pond, Hampton Bays

Peconic Lake

Canoe Lake, Riverhead

Swan Lake, Riverhead

Mackay Lake, Riverhead

Sandy Pond, Calverton

Fox Pond, Calverton

Linnus Pond, Calverton

Jones Pond, Calverton

Upper and Lower Lake, Yaphank

Carmen's River, Brookhaven

Artist Lake, Middle Island

Lake Panamoka, Ridge NY

Deep Pond, Ridge NY (Boy Scout Camp)

Big Fresh Pond, North Sea

Little Fresh Pond, North Sea

Long Pond on Sage Road, Greenport

Hook Pond, East Hampton

Fresh Pond, Amagansett/Heather Hills

Fort Pond, Montauk

Big Reed Pond, East Hampton

Montauk Point

Fresh Pond, Shelter Island

Trout Pond, Noyack

Avon Lake, Amityville

We love good fishing spots, and we love to add new ones to our list. Because there's always something alluring about new fishing spots. Early on, the boys and I would look on the local maps and attempt to go to the ponds or lakes or rivers. We attempted to go to every spot on the east end of Long Island. It was fun going to a new pond or lake.

As I was compiling this list, I had to get out a map to remember the names and areas. It's hard to believe there are that many ponds and lakes and fishing spots on Long Island. And this is not an exhaustive list. I started to write down the list a few weeks ago, and I didn't realize there were so many spots.

You'd think I just went fishing most of the time. Trips were mostly in the evening with the boys. Some were seasonal, especially on the bays and ocean, but they were some of the best ones. The most often fished places were close to home, easiest to get to. Most of the trips were by boat in lakes and ponds. As we grew in our bass master catalogs new techniques and baits, fishing line poles and reels, it broadened our fishing.

As time went by and the boys went to college, I started wader fishing more and more. I very much enjoyed that. I'd stop somewhere on the way home from a job and don waders and *make a few casts*. I'd be back on the road in less than a lunch break.

HAND FISHING FOR BLUEGILLS

This story starts at a favorite swimming and fishing spot, Laurel Lake, at the end of the summer. We went there with Sean, the *Salmon Dog*. You walk down a 200-yard path and into the water's sandy bottom. The water is very clear. It's always nice looking out over the 30-acre kettle pond, wooded nearly all the way around. I take my shoes off and get in with my pole but nothing is biting. The blue gills, however, are biting our toes. This is so unusual that I'm not even sure it is really happening. They weren't breaking the skin; it was more of an amusement, kind of funny. There are a lot of bluegills that hang out at the put-in spot every year. There is some cover for them along the shoreline. I'm kind of enjoying the attention.

Sean picks up a few muscles out of the sand and cracks them and scraps the meat out of them and holds the meat in his hand. He has the young blue gills, about three to four inches long, eating the muscles right out of his hand. They start swimming in and out of his hand, grabbing a piece and then darting back out a few inches. Then they would fight over the meat. It was nice to watch. It reminded me of feeding the animals at the zoo.

As Sean fed them more, they got less cautious. It's interesting how even though they are fish, their caution can be thrown to the wind just like animals at the park or in your backyard. As I'm enjoying this feeding of the fish, they gather more together, and Sean grabs one while it's feeding out of his hand. I thought he lucked out. He got some more muscles and caught another one with his hand. I thought I have to try this! I got some bluegills eating out of my hand, but I wasn't fast enough to grab them.

I always thought it would be a great thing to bring some kids down to Laurel Lake in the summer to have fish eating out their hands and maybe to catch a fish with their bare hands. Or maybe even some big kids.

GOING FOR ICE CREAM

I do like ice cream. It sometimes gives me stomach trouble. I had not had any for a while, so on the way to Little Giant to get some ice cream bars, I passed a spot where a man lets me fish in his pond. I've got a new truck he doesn't know, so I thought on the way back, I would make a quick stop so he would recognize my new truck. I drove down his driveway to the pond. It passes right by his house. So, I pick up the ice cream and eat one in the parking lot and head home. I pull into the driveway, and he's sitting there. I stop and introduce myself again and head to the back. I thought I would make a few casts, so I got out, grabbed my pole and walked over to the pond.

The water was down some, typically fall level. I'm looking up the pond towards where the water comes in, and there are a few trees down. I see some swirling in the water and a bunch of small bait fish. As I'm heading there, I notice some familiar ground cover that's nice to walk on. It's got to be eight inches tall. It has a beautiful pink color to it. It's as soft as I remember it. I didn't really want to walk on it because it had got tall, and I and I didn't want to mess it up. I catch one small bass, and I'm walking in the Japanese straw grass working my way to the downed tree.

At the water's edge, I see a turtle trying to grab a frog, a big frog. The turtle is winning. He slides back off the bank with the frog in his beak. I move closer to the downed tree. Another frog is trying to make his way to the pond. It is jumping over the deep grass to get there. I like that. I'm at the down tree. There's nothing there, but there's a duck nesting house, and there's often a bass hanging there. Nope. Not today. I'm looking to the other side, and I see a bass jump close to the shore. I'm getting a little excited.

I cross the end of the pond. It looks passable despite the deep grass. There's a dock ramp in the water. There are usually fish there. I make a few casts and get stuck. I change direction and get my line out of the dock walkway. I look across to the other side. I'm going to try. I step out of the grass into the pond bottom and sink up to my hips. I step in with my other foot thinking maybe I can walk out.

Nope.

When I try to move, my new sneakers are coming off in the mud. As my fishing pole is stuck in the mud, reel first, it comes to my mind "how am I going to get out of here?" I'm a mess. I look around for something in the grass — hidden in the grass is a limb sticking up just level with the grass.

God has made a way of escape for me.

I'm wondering if the branch is going to hold me. It did. I was able to pull myself out of this predicament I was in.

There was a spiritual lesson here — all the trouble I get in, but God never leaves me nor forsakes me, but provides a way of escape. I was surprised at the branch right where it needed to be and all the warnings I didn't heed. But there was a way out, and I did not provide it.

SEINE NETS

Jacking eels goes way back to my childhood at
Amityville Beach, netting them with a seine net that we
had. It was eight feet long and three feet high sticks on
each end to hold the net top and bottom. The net had
quarter-inch holes with small floats on the top and lead
weights on the bottom. I loved doing this. You never
knew what kind of fish you were going to catch. Small eels,
four or five inches long, got caught in the net sometime,
too. I should back up here a little.

We first started seining for fish with a beach
towel. Mom would let us use an old one. There would
always be someone trying to catch something at the beach,
and there would be a few kids gathered when they brought
in the net to see what they got — maybe a few killies or
silversides or a small crab or a jellyfish or a small eel. I
really enjoyed doing that. I still would enjoy doing that. I
remember when my father got the real seine net. He used
to keep it on the boat, so we could catch bait to catch
snappers. We used it more for fun to see what kind of
creatures were around there.

There was a sand bar by West Gilgo that was
formed when they dredged the State Channel. We used to
stay on the south side of the sandbar where a small bay

formed. It was a nice spot to swim and catch something in the seine net. As I think back, whoever was around when you did this would gather and wait to see what you got. Sometimes they'd handle the little fish.

One day, I remember we were with my brother Brian who is four years older than I am. We had some killies and silversides in the net. Brian was talking about eating the fish raw. Some people do that as a routine all over the world, he said. So, he was biting into them and eating them. Not to be left out, I tried to eat a silverside raw. It was very salty, and that was good, but I couldn't get past the raw fish taste or the idea. I remember telling people about that decades later — standing on the shore of the bay, with the catch bubbling around us in the seine net, and scooping fish from the net to eat raw with my big brother.

I remember clearly how we dragged the seine net up onto the beach, and the water drained out almost instantly, and then the net came alive with fish, flipping all over the place.

The spectators would make *ohhhs* and *ahhs* over it. Me, too.

EELING IN THE GREAT SOUTH BAY

When I was a kid, jacking at night was just about
the most exciting thing a boy could do with his dad. I
know it was mine. I remember always asking in the
afternoon "could we go eeling tonight," and my dad would
look up at the treetops. If the leaves were slightly moving,
and I mean slightly, we could not go. The water on the
Great South Bay would ripple and we would not be able to
see the bottom and the eels. I would protest, "Come on!
Let's go anyway." I learned a lot about eeling in those days.

My dad had a 16-foot lapstrake boat with a 25-
horsepower Evinrude, a Coleman lantern with two
mantels, a burlap bag, and a spear. Dad had a nice spear. It
was hand forged, eight prongs, barbed slightly with a
twelve-foot wooden pole. We would go out to the
cowyard. We would pole the boat along the edge with the
light positioned along the front. You would get up on the
front seat and get ready for the eels on the bottom
slithering around.

You tried first to catch them at the far edge of the
light so they wouldn't bolt. It was better if the tide was half
tide going out, so the water was not deep. It was easier to
spear them if it was not too deep. It was harder to judge
with the light where they were exactly. My early days as a

kid, I would miss a lot. You don't really throw the spear; you let it slide out of your hand. When it gets close, you push down and aim for the head. Very exciting, just thinking about it gets me excited. When you've got one, they squirm all over the place and you have to get them off the spear. They will bite you if they have the opportunity.

This is when it got even more exciting — trying to get the eel in the burlap bag. They are very, very slimy and when they get in the bag you can pull them off the spear. Once in a while, they'd get loose on the bottom of the boat, and you had to try to grab them with a rag and get them back in the burlap bag. I loved jacking at night. I loved eeling. They are a worthy opponent. I loved looking at the bottom to see what's down there and still do. I knew when I got older, I was going to get all the stuff to go jacking at night, and I did. But that's another story or two.

THE CORRAL
Newnan, GA

I had the privilege to take part in ministering to handicapped kids at the Corral in Newnan, Ga, not far from my house. It started out a few months ago when Faith Bible Church Men's Group had a Men's Take Your Children Fishing event one Saturday. I'm always looking for fishing spots, so I'm going to go over there Saturday morning. I knew the name of it, but I wasn't sure where it was. I got close. There's a small sign on the corner of the road. I wasn't sure what property it was. I drove down the block. It did not look like a place to go fishing. I drove back around, and went down another side street and saw a pond down in the hollow. I turned around and went back and there were a few vehicles parked on the grass next to a barn. I didn't want to give up looking for the pond. I pulled in, parked on the grass, and started walking down. That's when I saw people fishing, a bunch of fathers and sons.

The Corral has three docks/decks built on the pond — easy to fish. You can fish the whole shoreline. It's a nice place. I met the owner/operator. He had five kids that he was baiting poles for. He was also unhooking fish for them as they caught fish. I met James fishing at the dam as I was walking around the pond. I had a nice chat with him. His boys were catching fish. I moved to the far side where I sat down on a chair on the deck at the water's edge with a person I recognized from church and his son. They were catching and keeping fish to take home. They were enjoying themselves, and I was enjoying the conversation. They were using floats to fish. While I was sitting there, one went under. I thought how excited they got and me too when the float went under. I still get excited when that happens, and so do most people. It really doesn't matter how many times it happens. It's like turning on a light switch. You just get excited. I had a nice chat with his son and headed along the pond. There was some nice greenery along the way. I didn't bring my fishing pole.

I had a nice morning, so my thought was that I had to come back again when no one was here. Maybe in the evening. I came by three times to talk to the owner and see if I could fish here. I spoke with James at the church. He didn't know the owner. James said I had to talk to Les about it. I didn't know who that was, so a week went by. Turns out Les was the father I sat with at the dock. He asked me to do a little plumbing job for him. He knew the owner at Corral. Les spoke with him and set me up to come fishing on Wednesdays from 10-12 to help handicapped kids. That way Les thought I could get to know him myself and set up my own time to go fish alone.

It's kind of a long story, but as I look back, I think maybe it was ordained for me to go help handicapped kids to fish. The real blessing was coming. I wasn't sure about helping handicapped kids. Could I do it right? Whatever right is. I get there at 10am on Wednesday. Another man and I are manning one of the decks. The kids come in on a bus. There were six or seven kids with their teacher coming to our deck. No instructions, no rules — just let's go fishing using worms. I can do that. They all wanted to fish— perfect. And they were catching sunnies pretty quickly and a few catfish.

It was Lilla's turn to fish. She was excited. We had another young lady put the worm on for Lilla. Lilla had the pole over the rail, and she sang out in the sweetest, prettiest voice, loudly, "Here fishy, fishy, fishy! Here fishy, fishy, fishy!" It was a call from the past over half a century ago. I heard that fish call off the back of *Betty Ann* in the state channel in Amityville, New York, by Rudy Sittler. I was stunned. Then, too, I was taken aback and stunned. But Lilla's call was much sweeter and more honest. She had never caught a fish. She caught two.

What a blessing to be here with Lilla catching her first fish and that call of hers, "Here fishy, fishy." I could never have planned this. God is good!

BLUEFISH

I was taking a walk this morning — a beautiful fall morning — the colors are just stunning. The reds — I can't remember them being more beautiful. Also, the yellows are gleaming in the trees. It's the kind of morning that gets you reflecting. Remembering bygone days. I'm thinking about fishing. That's not unusual, but this morning I'm thinking of fishing for bluefish in the fall off the Long Island Sound. They are quite the predators and great fighters on hook and line. In the summer, if you live anywhere by salt water and have a fishing pole, you fish for snappers. We would troll for them with my dad off the state channel. They were easy fish to catch, and there were lots of them. My mom would cook them in bacon fat. They were about ten inches long, and she would serve them to the family sometimes. Now and again, we would catch a cocktail blue, 15 or 16 inches. Out in the ocean once, in my younger days on a party boat, we caught a bunch of blues with chunks of meat on a hook. It was a hoot.

When we moved out east with the family and started fishing more and learning the how-tos of fishing on the beach and what's running in each season, I learned to wait and watch for the bluefish coming around Long

Island Sound from up north on their way south. That was when I got the right equipment, a longer pole with thicker, heavier line, and a steel leader. The boys and I looked forward to fishing off the beach.

The most exciting thing was watching the blues moving along the beach working their way down to where you were waiting. If there was a north wind blowing, we knew to go out and watch for the bait fish bringing the blue fish into the shore. Once it started to happen, there were many points along the beach to watch and fish for bluefish. The anticipation of them coming along the shore line could drive you crazy.

Sometimes I was so excited about getting out of the truck that I could hardly tie the hook onto the line. The birds would work around them eating small chunks of bait fish that the blue fish crunched up. Sometimes you would see a seagull missing a foot because it got too close to the feeding frenzy. That's what we liked. The feeding frenzy in the fall on the beach and waiting for a school to pass by twenty feet from shore.

After work one day, Tom and I were at a Long Island Sound beach in Green Point called Sixty-Seven Steps Beach by Horton's Lighthouse. It has a long set of steps down to the beach (but not 67). We were fishing to the left of the stairs. There were lots of boulders and rocky shores. A few massive boulders sat in the water not far out. I was throwing a swim bait and hooked onto a nice one. I dragged it to shore and had it on the beach.

There were a couple of fellows, I think a Dad and son. The father couldn't speak English. The son asked what we were going to do with the fish. I said let him go. He asked if he could have the fish. I said yes. I was glad to give it to him. It was in the sand, and the father was touching him around the mouth. His mouth was open, and I yelled at him not to stick his fingers in the fish's mouth!

Too late.

The fish clamped down and the father pulled to get his fingers out of its mouth. It was all bloody. After a few minutes, his son asked if there was a hospital around here, and I told him where it was. He needed one. I learned for sure that day, don't stick your fingers in a live bluefish's mouth. Their teeth are very sharp. They never give up. They fight the whole way.

TOOT

Toot was my firstborn. Jacki was in labor for 24 hours. It was back in 1978. Katherine was born on my mom's birthday on May 28, springtime in New York. Life would never be the same. I remember how excited I was when she was born: Katherine Perrine Baxter came into the world!

I remember going over to Mom's that night and telling her about Katherine being born. We gave our baby girl my mom's mother's name and my wife's grandmother's name. I just wasn't prepared for the miracle of life; it seems like yesterday.

Now let me explain why I call Katherine *Toot* — not spelled right but that's the way it has gone. They tried to correct me, but it stuck. When *Toot* was very small, she would sit on my lap at the player piano, and I would sing to her *Toot Toot Tootsie Don't Cry*. This was something we did a lot when she was little. Eventually I started calling her *my Toot*. My family doesn't correct me anymore, and the rest of the family on occasion call her *Toot* too.

I don't sing the song from Al Jolson *Toot Toot Tootsie Don't Cry* any more, but I still call her *my Toot* and always will.

VIVIAN

All that the sun shines on is beautiful, so long as it is wild.
~John Muir

The meaning of Vivian's name — alive and lively from the French. Children are treasures even when that's clouded by life. The beauty that lies in these little faces can make a grown man cry.

I remember when Katherine came to tell me and Jacki that she was going to call her baby Vivian. I thought, "Vivian?"

It didn't seem quite right—it was different, not the mainstream, not normal. But it is all those things and more. I came to love that name. She is so cute.

I have a picture of Vivian in my head. She's picking a dandelion on her front lawn in New Jersey. She was only eight-months old. These must be some of her first steps; she wears a white bonnet, and holds a small pail in her right arm firmly wedged all the way up to her elbow, with those baby pudgy arms. She leans forward with her knees bent reaching out with her left hand to grab the seed pod of a dandelion.

What a beautiful picture — moment — a special moment — a first pick — a dandelion. The way — a place we all came from — the attraction — the wonder— the newness — the doing outside — the beginning — the promise — the hope — the beauty — what a sight — Life — the start.

I love the photo. She's so cute that I can hardly take it all in. I originally had the photo on my phone and kind of forgot it. I looked at it and thought about it as I thought about grandkids. It somehow went missing. I tried to find it, but I wasn't able to retrieve it despite all the ways I tried. But the image is burned on my memory, and I fondly bring it up from time to time.

I thank God for little kids. They are so, so cute, especially when they are yours.

MARK BAXTER, DECEMBER 12, 2023

Life begins for my grandson. There's so much to think about. What does it mean to be a grandfather? What's your job? What should I be thinking about?

That it's a blessing to be one. Children are a gift from God. They truly are. I believed that when my children were born and still do. <u>Gifts</u>. We've all been given gifts: mental ability, physical ability, to understand, to care for others. When I look at Marky, I think about what he might be when he grows up. What can I do in the raising of that boy, even at my age? He is growing fast. He's almost three months old. I was thinking about that the other day while I was on the way home from visiting him. I was riding down Senoia Road, a short cut under Hwy 74. I wanted to see a particular tree that was blooming. A tree. It is springtime. I love springtime, my favorite time of the year. Everything is new, coming to life, born again, like the birth of a child.

This spring brought the infancy of a child, and he is blooming. This spring brings my rebirth as a grandfather, and this time I can be present in the life of my grandson. I stop at this blooming tree, and I feel compelled to get out and look. I pull over, get out, and as I get closer, it's so beautiful. Stunning. I look it up on my phone app to identify it. It's a Sanger Magnolia. I'm thinking, I'm going to have to bring Marky here every Springtime to enjoy this together and talk about things.

Also, it's Spring and daffodils are all around. I've been looking for the nicest and biggest patches. I found one on Hwy 29. That's the biggest I've found but they are all around. Marky, you've got to have your eyes open. I need to show him all the beaver woodwork that I'm so enamored with. It seems to be all over this part of Georgia. There's also a deep ruby azalea here that is getting ready to bloom. My favorite color. The beauty and the glory that is here, I hope I am able to share and instill this love of nature in you. Because, Marky, it's all around us to see and take in.

I hope I get to go fishing with Marky and his dad in Grandma Fay's boat. Just the thought of that is great!

Every day, I sit in my recliner, and I watch as the digital frame rotates through the pictures my family and I love. I see the pictures of Tom and Sean when they were small. And pictures of fishing trips in Grandma Fay's boat. I love those boys and the memories we have made together. I hope Marky and I have the same relationship. I hope I live long enough to enjoy that. If not, my grandsons Evan and Marky will have my wishes and my thoughts and the idea of a beautiful tree in springtime.

THE ONE THAT GOT AWAY

Many years ago, I read a story in a sporting magazine, *Field and Stream*, suggesting that stories about the fish that got away could be the best fishing stories of all. I was quite sure that could not be, but as the years went by, and I took more and more fishing trips with my boys, such a trip stands out as one that made me rethink this.

The trip started on late August day with my two sons, Tom and Sean, and their cousin, Jeff. They were around twelve or thirteen. Tom and Sean wanted to take Jeff fishing. Tom had a new bait-casting reel, a first for us because we usually use spinning reels. The bait casting reels are hard to get used to. We didn't bring the boat, so they were fishing from the shore.

I had to meet someone, so I left the boys at the pond. It was before cell phones, so I told them I'd come back to take them home later. When I came back two hours later, the boys weren't there. Jacki had come to get them. I drove home and when I walked into the house, the boys were sitting close together quietly in the living room. I was thinking "how could you get in trouble fishing?"

Then they started talking, Sean first, talking about the big fish Tom had on. Tom started telling me how he had his pole leaning on the cattails and all of a sudden, his pole was crashing through the cattails toward the water. Tom grabs the pole, and the fish is taking line off the reel. He starts fighting the fish trying to reel it in. It gets close to shore, and there's a lot of weeds, so Jeff grabs the line. Experienced fishermen know to never grab the line when you're fighting a fish, especially a big one.

The line breaks, and Sean jumps in the water and grabs the fish into his arms — a big one — a ten pounder, they say. Sean wrestles with it trying to get it to shore. But seconds later, it's gone. He just couldn't hold on to it. The fish was gone, but the story wasn't.

They so much loved telling me that story, and I so much-loved hearing it. The fish that got away can be the best fishing story, and it was.

DANDELIONS

A flowering plant belonging to the Asteraceae family derived from the French phrase dent de lion which means "lion's teeth." The shape of the plant's flowers resembles a lion's tooth.

We often called it a puff ball. Every part of it is edible, a lot of vitamin C and medicinal purposes. Living in suburbia, when I grew up, all the kids around knew about Dandelions, the puff balls, especially when they were ripe. We would blow on them and the seeds would go everywhere; we would even blow them on each other and have puff ball fights. Handling the yellow flowers, you would get yellow on your hands. One of my favorite photos is of my granddaughter picking one. It was the first flower she picked.

But at last, the dandelion was a curse to suburbia. It would grow everywhere, lawns, gardens, edges, curbs. So, my father and the other fathers would go to great lengths to get rid of them. I remember that one of my chores was to remove the dandelions by pulling them out. I remember my father saying, "you've got to get the roots out or they will grow back." It was hard getting the root out. My father had a spreader that he would use to spread chemicals to kill them. Before the chemicals, dandelions would take up a lot of room on the lawn. One time, my father put too many chemicals out and almost killed the whole lawn.

I would just mow them with the grass. I guess I was led to believe that you had to get rid of dandelions. I didn't think that much of them until I moved out east. I would see the Greek people picking them in the Springtime, just the leaves. We kind of would make fun of them eating dandelions. They spent quite a lot of time picking them along the sides of the road. Nobody bothered them. It was like they were doing a public service by getting rid of the dandelions.

I remember one day when I was in my forties driving the main road in Southold looking out on a farm field, and as far as the eye could see, there were dandelions in full bloom. It was beautiful, stunning. Can I say showstopping? I had to call my mom and tell her how beautiful the dandelions were in that field. She wasn't excited but was glad to hear from me and pleased that I was so excited. I remember thinking, "I'm going to have to rethink Dandelions, their value and worth." That started me thinking about other things that I had learned and might need to rethink.

ANSWERED PRAYERS

I remember when Jacki was pregnant with Katherine, and the time was close for her birth, I would go fishing now and again at Avon Pond. There was something in the air — anticipation — something big was about to happen. I didn't really have words for it or really understand it. The day came, and I remember being in the hospital. We had been to Lamaze classes, and I tried to do the breath coaching. I don't think I was much help. But the time came, and Katherine was born. Truly — I was excited, surprised, and astonished — A baby! My baby! Our baby! A miracle of miracles. I was so excited — it started to sink in. A baby, and she was so beautiful. I was smitten. To make it even more miraculous, she was born on my mom's birthday. I will never forget that.

I was startled by the intensity of the love I had for this child born to us. It was the same when the boys were born. All those feelings happened again for Tom and Sean, but by then I knew to expect it. Life as I had never seen it before. Having children changed me. I remember years later, after they had grown into childhood, thinking about them and deciding that I didn't want to foul it up. That's happened to so many families. They don't talk to each other. In my own family those problems exist, but I didn't want that to happen with my children.

I remember praying for my children and praying that we would have healthy conversations and still love one another. I still do. I remember listening to a sermon on family relationships. It was about spending time with your children and doing things together. This doesn't seem that hard, really. So, for my sons, I took up fishing. It took on a life of its own. But it started with a prayer to my Great God who heard and answered that prayer.

I probably would not even remember it, but looking at all these fishing pictures and telling all these fishing stories, God brought to memory a prayer he answered some thirty-five years ago and is still answering even to this day. We still love each other, and we're still talking. Sometimes we even go fishing. Praise God.

PRIZED POSSESSIONS

We all have prized possessions. It's not something that I think about very much. I have a lot of possessions. I was telling my wife that I was going to write a story about my prized possession. She wanted to know if I was going to write about my fishing poles. No, I like them, but they don't come up to being prized possessions.

I'm thinking about that word "prized." I think about all that I've been blessed with. There really is a long list. Writing these stories has reminded me of so many good memories, and they are prized. I think of pictures of Katherine's children—the one of Vivian with her hat on picking the dandelions. I think of saying hello to them every morning as if they were here with me. I cherish my ability to pray for them at every meal. I prize that Tom and Maria are having a baby boy. Such a blessing! Sean and Ankana are looking for a house to buy in Florida. I pray for them all — for their salvation and their lives.

Of course, these relationships aren't possessions the same way an object is, but I value them above all.

However, there is a little story about my prized possession. The first thought of this came many years ago when I began plumbing. I remember installing a cast iron tub. It was a hard job as the tub was so heavy. I thought one day, when I got some money or enough money, I'm going to get one of those cast iron tubs — the big one, the wide one, the deep one. I thought at the time, that would be the cat's meow!

We built a house for our family, and I had a six-foot fiberglass whirlpool tub installed. It wasn't the same. It was nice, but it wasn't a Kohler Mendota, 5-foot-long, 32 inches wide, 11-inches deep, white, cast iron tub.

Fast forward 35 years, when we were looking for a house in Georgia and came to see a home at 55 Harbor View. I remember looking in the bathroom, and there it was — a Kohler 5-foot-long, 32 inches wide, 11 inches deep, and white. It was like new. The couple never used the bathroom on the other end of the house. I remembered that day so long ago when I said I wanted one someday. Maybe someday was here.

We bought the house. It's a beautiful house, the nicest place we've ever lived. I started using the shower in that bathroom, but eventually I used the tub. And I haven't looked back. Sometimes I take a bath every night. It really cleans you, soaking like that. It helps with muscles and aches. I really love getting that white cast iron Kohler tub clean and shiny. You know the way some people love keeping their new cars pristine, that's how I feel about my tub. I think I'm going to use my prize possession now.

HIBISCUS

This story is about the Hibiscus, a plant in the evergreen shrub family. They are a symbol of positivity and cheer. They have some of the biggest flowers on them, and the most blooms of flowering bushes. And the flowers only last a day — oh what a beautiful day!

My first introduction to hibiscus flowers was in Bermuda on our honeymoon. We have a picture of Jacki wearing one over her ear. It's one of my favorite photos.

We had some hibiscus in New York, so we got some here. We got one last year that was eaten by deer pretty badly and five smaller ones this year. But as the plants flowered, deer ate the tops. So, I was going to make a concerted effort to protect the one I purchased last year. There were no flowers on that one.

I went around and put new batteries on the motion detectors. I've got five of them now. And I bought another gallon of Deer Away and sprayed more than they recommended. I also used a granule deterrent on the ground. I was going to get a fence around the Hibiscus, but the deterrent seemed to be keeping the deer at bay. I've been keeping a close eye on the damage on the hibiscus.

Well, today is Father's Day. I got up at 7 o'clock, and I looked out the front window over the front lawn. I wanted to see if it got any greener after I fertilized it — Maybe a little. The rain we had this week helped for sure. A lot of people want to have a green and lush lawn. I guess I kinda do too, even though I like the weeds more sometimes.

I also noticed a dead squirrel in the street. I've been noticing a lot of squirrels being run over.

Now I'm off to the kitchen to make a cup of coffee. As always, I'm looking at the birdbath to see if the bees are there. I look at the feeders to see if they need to be filled.

And there below the feeder facing this way — And I mean facing this way — on Father's Day — is a big beautiful red hibiscus, the first flower on the hibiscus to bloom.

It would be nice any day, but on Father's Day, it was so nice. It comes by a Fatherly hand who upholds and directs everything for his glory. Praise God for his gifts, my creator and sustainer.

AN ENCOUNTER WITH A RACCOON FAMILY AT THE WATERING HOLE

One evening in late summer, some years back at one of my favorite ponds, the shore line was dried up as it is every year at this time. One of my favorite places to fish in Long Island is in an old farm field, half overgrown. There is nobody around, and you are all by yourself. It's really a nice place to be. I usually go for an hour, once around the pond.

On this day, as I make my way around in waders, I notice some movement in the bushes up in front of me on the side of a small drainage ditch. Suddenly, a small head pops out. It's a raccoon, maybe 30 feet away, watching me. I am a little surprised because this has never happened before, and then she's gone. I thought that was cool. It seemed a couple of minutes, and then I heard rustling in the bushes. Three small kits came rolling out, tumbling out of the bushes, climbing on each other, biting one another, and just having a good time. I felt blessed to be there; I could stop right here, but there is more.

All of a sudden, mom shows up and makes some mom-racoon-screeching noise, and those three juveniles snapped to, lined up behind their mom, and off they went down the shoreline with the kids in line, so to speak. As I think about it, I always see this as a divine appointment. I am amazed how animal moms and human moms have the mothering instinct. You see that all through the animal world.

BEAGLE FOR OUR LUNCH

This took place in early spring at one of our favorite ponds, Swan Pond in Calverton, New York. It's in the pine barrens in the center of Eastern Long Island in the Peconic River Basin, a forty-minute ride from our house. It's kind of a remote and undeveloped part of Long Island. Swan Pond has a lot of lily pads which was a very attractive fish-holding feature and why we liked it so much. I think the area around Swan Pond was a private club at one time, and there's a small house on the property.

Tom and I were working in Ridge that day. Normally I would skip lunch and work on through, but when Tom was working with me, he'd fuss about skipping lunch. Eventually, I relented, and it turned out that having lunch was always a good thing. Tom got me to change my pattern, and I'm grateful for that.

On coming home that day, we stopped at a MacDonald's for lunch and got some hamburgers and fries. I thought we would stop at Swan Pond on the way home and see what was going on around there. The Swan Pond area is loaded with ponds that feed into a major river, the Peconic River. We canoed different sections of the river, and that area was a favorite spot to find new places to fish. When we got close on River Road, Tom yelled out, "Stop the truck! Stop the truck!" There were two beagles at the wood's line along the road, right next to the lake.

We pulled over and Tom jumped out and was trying to catch one. One of them would have no part of Tom, but the other one would. Tom picked him up and brought him into the truck. I was ready to break out lunch. I started opening my hamburger, and the dog climbed up my arm to get it. And I mean climbed! He was diligent. My first impulse was to stop him, but I thought for a moment and realized, "He's way hungrier than me!" He took my hamburger and gulped it down. I can't remember ever meeting a dog that hungry.

As I was looking through the pictures of fishing adventures recently, I came across a picture of Tom in his Yankee jacket holding the dog. Tom is a big Yankee fan! I looked at the dog's face and for the first time, I saw on that beagle's face "Take me home." I remember Tom wanted to also. I kind of did, too. We already had a couple of dogs at the time. We took him to the pound. Hopefully, his owner found him there.

A VISIT FROM A BALD EAGLE

This story starts when I was cleaning up some brush and small trees on the side of the yard in Southold, New York, many years ago.

There were some healthy-looking plants growing in that small, wooded area. It was springtime, and they looked promising. There were quite a few of them. When they got bigger, I discovered that they were common Groundsel which is a small plant that endangered bumble bees like. So, I let them grow. They got white paint brush-like flowers on them. As the year went by, those small, endangered bees showed up. I remember being thrilled going outside and looking at the bees enjoying those plants. There must have been about two dozen of those plants that most people would have considered weeds to be culled.

At the same time, I was reading a *Field and Stream* magazine, and they were speaking about how to trim and maintain woods and woodlots. It was an interesting article. One of the things they talked about was what trees you should leave and not cut down. It was the dead ones—the ones that had lots of holes in them from bugs and birds, no bark—in other words, the first ones that you'd want to cut down. The article explained how those kinds of trees are a home to a vast amount of animal life and productive to the woods, like the common groundsel is to bees.

I had one of those trees in this small piece of woods to the south side of the house. Yes, there was no bark, and yes, there were bugs in it. Yes, it was dead as a doornail. It looked like a piece of driftwood standing there against all the healthy green trees. Yes, my family often reminded me that it wasn't attractive. I could see their point, but it had some beauty to me now because I knew the role it served in the woods. I got a lot of guff like "Dad, what are you losing your mind? You're leaving a dead tree out there." It must have been before Hurricane Sandy because that tree would not have survived the hurricane. You could press against it, and it would sway.

That fall, Jacki called me from the kitchen. She was excited, saying, "There's a bald eagle in the backyard?" "No way, where is it? " I asked. We'd heard there was a family of Bald Eagles nesting east of us at Orient Point. Everybody was excited about that and wanted to see them. I wanted to see them because they are the symbol of our country and the land I love.

I was thinking about all of that—how much I love America and how much I love the woods and the water and the wildlife—as I ran out and looked over the backyard. The bald eagle was sitting in the dead tree I left.

From that perch he could look out across the whole of Goose Creek.

Whatever attracted him to that dead tree attracted me, too — the deadness, the bugginess, the brownness, the unobstructed view all around and down the creek.

That tree, like the common groundsel, has shaped my idea of beauty.

A THOUSAND SHADES OF GREEN

This story starts at Pepacton Reservoir in upstate
New York. It is the largest by volume of the New York
State water sources, some seventeen miles long and seven-
tenths of a mile wide. In scale it rivals the island of
Manhattan. In fact, 25% of New York City's drinking
water comes from Pepacton Reservoir.

We always pass by it on the winding road to Pine
Hill, Steve's Place. It's all tree lined so as you pass by you
only get glimpses of the water — very clean and pristine.
It flows on the stream bed of the east branch of the
Delaware River. So, the mountains that surround it rise up
from the water line. On this day, we are going to fish for
smallmouth bass. This is our third trip to fish the reservoir
in early June; however, we'd been there fishing streams at
other times of the year, dozens of times. We'd learned that
the fishing in early June can be excellent, so we came to
fish, me and my sons.

We have a boat at the reservoir bridge; it's a nice
spot to put in. You have to leave your boat there or every
time you take it out, you have to get it steam cleaned
before you put it back in. They also require aluminum
boats that are manually propelled and no longer than
fourteen feet. Our boat is not alone: there are aluminum

boats all along the reservoir upside down, sometimes tied to trees.

We start fishing down from the bridge and always going to the right, rowing, no motors here. We push off and paddle some distance then fish back to the shoreline. I'm there to fish like I have so many times before, but this time my eyes are drawn to the opposite shoreline, and I start looking up the wall of the mountain, noticing the many different trees — all trees I'd seen before, but I'd never noticed them like that. It was spectacular. I could hear my father's voice scolding me: "Baxter, you're not paying attention!" But this time I was paying attention.

I was startled by how they grew up right out of such a steep hillside. Some of the trees jutted out perpendicular and then righted themselves toward the sun. I started moving my eyes looking down the mountainside and all around me; it was stunning—all around 360 degrees. I'd been here many times before, but it was as if this was the first time that I'd really seen it.

John Muir, the American Naturalist, said, "It's not what you look at that matters, it's what you see." I'd looked at this view before, but I never saw it until that day. Where are the words I'm looking for? A thousand shades of green— I could not stop looking.

These are the things parents and grandparents must help their children to see, the beauty and the wonder that is all around.

BEAVER DAMS

The sounds of water running over

The different streams running over in different fashions

The light sparkling in different ways

The white water with air bubbles moving down

The sound, oh the sounds

To think a brown critter with a flat tail built that

You think not

But it's true

A miracle

Not any ordinary thing

May it never be

There all around you, you would never know

Can a rodent really build a damn?

Yes. What a great creator.

A SPRING DAY IN DECEMBER

The whole world is a series of miracles, but we're so used to them
we call them ordinary things.

~Hans Christian Anderson

I had a text from Sean. He had caught a nice
couple of bass. One was his first five-pounder in Florida.
It inspired me to go fishing. It was a beautiful day in
Georgia in the seventies.

I went to a pond that I have permission to fish
down the road a piece from my house. After a lot of rain,
the pond had nice access but in the woods. It's a four-acre
pond with access all the way around. The one side is open,
the other wooded. Pretty much all the leaves were off the
trees. I was making casts with Gary Yamamoto Senko
worms. There was not much going on. I got one hit by a
dock. I decided to move to the backside of the pond, the
wooded side, where there was a path in the woods. On
that side, I got one fish and had three more on by a
downed tree.

On my way back, I noticed, just up the hillside
from the path, a yellow dandelion with a six-inch stem
sticking up in the fall leaves a half foot above the forest
floor—bright yellow and out of place this time of year. It

had a beautiful hard-to-describe look in the all-brown leaves and pine needles. Nonetheless, there it was, proudly and radiantly yellow, weaving its way through all the tan and brown and dusty orange. I enjoyed it from many angles, taking my time to walk around and see it from each vantage point.

And then I picked it and brought it home. I didn't enjoy it nearly as much as I enjoyed seeing it on the forest floor. It was out of place on my kitchen countertop. But on the forest floor, it was a glorious thing.

SPRINGTIME

Springtime is my favorite season of the year; everything dead comes alive. It's spiritual in nature; it's like being born again. It starts off slow and increases daily. I'm always looking in my travels for new things: flowering leaves starting to bud, so many different shades and hues of colors. I try to call the colors, but it's futile. I've tried in the past to look up colors online, but there's just too many. I thought, in the not-too-distant past, that the Crayola crayon box had them all. Nope. That's not true.

This has been an especially special spring. I had cataract surgery on both eyes. I really didn't realize how bad they were. It's been like a miracle, truly. Everything is more vibrant, clear, more vistas and long-distance views. Everything looks new, and I don't need glasses except for reading. And even that is better, too. So, I'm looking more because I'm seeing more. So, this is what got me thinking about writing this spring story.

This time of the year, it's also Spring cleanup and garden and trimming and taking stock of what's happening and what needs to be done. Jacki does most of that, which leads us usually to Lowes and Home Depot to look at flowering plants and bulbs — a nice time. This year Jacki got some flowers for the front flower boxes, a climbing rose bush, and a few others. Also, one peony plant which she planted right in front of our kitchen table where there's a big window. You can see the garden very well from there.

So, the peony was planted with hope that it would do well. It had one white flower with a streak of pink and a yellow center, but it was kinda droopy. We had a lot of rain after it was planted and it really took hold. That white and pink flower with the yellow center became vibrant there in the spring garden. I enjoyed looking at it every morning, and it seemed to get prettier every day. I was really getting to love that flower.

Then one morning I looked out, and the petals had all fallen off except one. I was sad, and I was surprised that I was sad. I was looking for some resolve to make sense of it all.

This is what came to mind:
"He has scattered the evidences of creation's former glories across the entire scape of heaven and earth and these evidences are also foretastes of the coming redemption of all things that those who live in this hard time between glories might see and remember, might see and take heart, might see and take the light in the extravagant beauty of bud and bloom knowing that these

living witnesses are rumors and reminders of a joy that will soon swallow all sorrow."

Hope of glory.

Quotation from *Every Moment Holy* by Douglas Kaine McKelvey

CRIMSON CLOVER

The very name sounds pretty: Crimson Clover. I long for springtime because I know one of my favorite flowers is Crimson Clover. We had a lot of rain this spring, and it's been good for all sorts of flowers, especially for the crimson clover.

I've been seeing some small patches along the highway, and I have a spot on the 34 Bypass where it fills the median in the middle down about a mile. I went by it at the beginning of the week. It's spectacular. The redtops, about a foot high, between four lanes of highway swaying in the wind—it just comes alive. I love looking at it. It's so pretty. It really is worth the trip just to drive by and see it.

I went by there on Wednesday just to cut a few pieces to bring to someone who loves plants and flowers, a small bunch. There were a few things that I noticed. The red on the clover was only half red. I thought to myself that it had more time to open and transform—more time to grow and beam. I thought more time, then, for me to enjoy it. The leaves had a pattern on them, a yellowish color. I don't remember seeing that before, so I thought maybe that was because of the spring rains.

I went to the bank on Saturday morning to do some banking before a trip to Hills and Dales Estate in LaGrange. The teller is a young lady and always asks me what I'm doing and where I'm going. So, I told her about the crimson clover and suggested that she go look at it. I told her how beautiful it is and where to find it. I piqued her interest.

I leave the bank on my way to Hills and Dales, a beautiful place with beautiful gardens. I'm looking forward to the drive. We're going to pass right by the patch of crimson clover. We hit Hwy 29 and turned onto 34. I look and look, but I don't see it. I think it must be further down. But it's not there.

They mowed it down!

There are just two or three stalks left, tucked against highway sign.

I'm calling my congressman.

WILDWOOD LAKE

Wildwood Lake in South Hampton, New York, is a natural spring-fed lake, 64 acres with a maximum depth of 60 feet. It is a nice place to take a swim, especially the deep part—cool and clean. They have a beach of sorts on the shallow end and lots of locals swim there. They have a rule that you have to have a local guide to take you there. I never did that. You must also be a resident of South Hampton. I'm not, but we fished there quite a bit. I would wader fish there, too.

I have a lot of fond memories there. The one I've been thinking about of late is my adventure with Sean in our new Jon Boat. It was not brand new, but it was new to us. No leaks and it fit in the back of the plumbing truck with the doors closed. I was a little concerned with its small size. I worried that it might not hold both of us safely. So, we went down to the Wildwood Lake which is a good clean lake to swim. We wanted to put the Jon Boat in to test it out, and that was going to involve getting in the water.

We put the Jon Boat in at the New York State access spot. We had an electric motor and battery, and we just started out going around the lake. I was in my fifties when we did this. It was a nice afternoon in late summer. I remember trying to see if we could sink it by hanging over the side or by both of us hanging over the side. Nope—it was very stable, surprisingly.

Sean jumped over and tried climbing back on— still good! And then I went over, both pulling on one side, still very stable. Sean spun the motor blade under the boat and turned the prop on from his position in the water. He had his legs stretched out behind him. I grabbed his big toes, and we motored across the pond—two grown men—Sean holding onto the shaft of the motor and me holding onto his big toes. I thought, "I'm a kid again," and I loved it.

Of course, it wasn't a wise idea, and it's not something I'd teach my grandchildren to do. But it was a good time, and I love thinking about that day at Wildwood Lake testing our new Jon boat. [OBJ]

THE SEWER JOB AND THE NATURE OF GOD

Who is God?

Genesis 1
God created the Heavens and Earth.

Acts 17:25
He himself gives everyone life and breath and everything else. He has no needs.

Proverbs 15:3
God sees all.

Hebrews 4:13
And no creature is hid from his sight.

Job 28:24
He looks to the ends of the Earth and sees everything.

First John 3:1
Children of God

Ephesians 2:10
We are his workmanship created for good work.

Isaiah 41:10
Fear not for I am with you.

Psalm 1: 39
Every one of my days were written in your book.
Romans 8:28
All things work together for good.

Colossians 2:4

My sins have been nailed to the cross.

Job 34:12
For his eyes are on the ways of a man and he sees all his steps.

Hebrews 4:12
For the word of God is living and active, sharper than any two-edged sword.

Philippians 3:20
But our citizenship is in Heaven, and from it we await a savior, the Lord Jesus Christ.

Psalm 139:24
Lead me in the way everlasting.

As this sewer job at my church comes to a close, I think back to what happened as I usually do on jobs like this. I don't remember one quite like this — with circumstances like this. The buildup to it was long, very long, too long. At my age, I'm not the man I once was in personal strength– where I could just depend on it. I know now that this is true, but in a lot of ways that's good because I need the Lord's strength and spirit work to calm me and guide me through. It caused me to cast my cares upon him for he cares for me. I think I want to control the situation in life and realizing we're responsible, and God is sovereign, is a very high truth. But realizing or considering God's sovereignty brings much more comfort and strength for me. I think the words of scripture are for me. I need to be meditating on them so much more as I see the day approaching.

One of the things that stands out on this sewer job is that it took five months to do two days' worth of work because of permitting and paperwork—there's something wrong about that.

The day of the job came early, 7 am. John was there and waiting for Tuthill, the directional-bore man. It started with a prayer for strength from John. I am aware of so many things that can go wrong. The excavator was very good. I was thankful to see that right away. I was hoping that I had the right fittings to do the hookup. As with real-life there are difficulties, but we overcame them. Praise God. I remember after the pipe was run, 400 feet, and John turned on the pump, waiting to see if it worked. It seemed like it took forever. I was thinking there must be something wrong. Ye of little faith. It finally started coming out of the new pipe at the manhole. Praise God. The inspectors were good, too. It works. I was excited. We finished by 3pm.

I remember doing sewer work in the past—if you finished early, things went well. And they did. Praise God. I stopped at the church office a few days later to drop off the piping material bills. In speaking with Kathy about the job, what had transpired—kind of like an after-the-game recap. As we were discussing it, I realized that the church never closed, never stopped ministering. There was a wedding there, 300 people, and all the other ministering that went on over the five months. During that time, they had to pump the tank twice a week. The Ministry went on, nonetheless. I think of the bible verse, "And the gates of Hell shall not prevail against it." It continued on. Praise God.

MILKWEED

My first encounter with Milkweed was in the early 1960s in Ketcham's Creek in New York. As a young boy, I loved going to the swamp and pond areas around us. I still do. I met up with the milkweed growing on the edge of Ketcham Creek, and I didn't like it. It was very sappy and sticky. It had flowers, and I guess when I tried to pick the flowers, I encountered the sticky stuff. After that, I stayed away from it.

Nearly half a century later, I reencountered Milkweed. I was fishing in one of my favorite ponds. I didn't have my waders on that day. So, I was making my way around a Riverhead pond through the brush. There were a few spots around that pond where I could get close to the edge of the pond. On my way around, I could see a patch of milkweed, well off the pond. It was loaded with pods, so I thought I would pick some and take them home.

I kept some in the ashtray of my truck and some on my desk at home. I thought at the time, what a mess that patch of milkweed was in that area of the pond — pods all over the place. So, when I got home, I read up on Milkweed, and it was very interesting. Especially the relationship between the milkweed and the Monarch butterfly. I thought maybe I could grow some milkweed and have monarch butterflies come visit the house. I'd read that Milkweed is the only thing they eat. It'd be awesome.

Come spring, I planted some outside the house, but it didn't come up. I thought maybe there wasn't enough sun. In other places in the yard, no luck. I remember stopping at a light in Southold. It was a beautiful day, no wind. I had my milkweed pods in my cup holder, they had started breaking open. I thought to myself, it's time to get rid of these. The experiment hadn't worked to grow them at home. It's time to let go, I thought.

The window of the van was open as I looked at the milkweed seeds in my hand. I hadn't noticed a breeze, but suddenly the wispy seeds, little puffs of cotton, flew from my hand like a bird, out and over the hood of the van into the distance. In the slightest breeze, I realized they could fly. Amazing that I got to witness that at a stop light in Southold. I still think of the design of those seeds — how can such a thing be lifted up and fly?

Later that year, I decided they were taking up too much space in the ashtray of my van. I also still had them on my desk. They were popping out of the pods and making a big mess. Again, it was time to really let go of the milkweed. I threw the rest of the seeds and the pods out the front window of my office into the garden bushes.

After that, I forgot about them. I'm not going to be able to grow them here, I thought. But by late spring, there were half-a-dozen milkweed plants blooming in the yard. I don't think my wife liked it. It didn't have that manicured garden look to it.

But it had my pond look to it!

LITTER AND TRASH

Roman 1:20
*For since the creation of the world, God's invisible qualities, his
eternal power, and divine nature have been clearly seen being
understood from what has been made.*

I have an ongoing struggle with litter and trash.
It's hard to come to grips with it. Why? Why? Why?

I think there's not one answer to that question.
The older I get the more it disturbs me. I think my stint in
the military established some groundwork for liking things
clean. I often explain that being in the service business and
cleaning people's houses after I'm done working is a very
important part of the job. My mom was a very clean
person. She always had the house clean with little help
from the rest of us. So, I think this is the foundation for
why I don't like litter around especially when I go fishing.
It pollutes the experience.

Over the last forty years or so, I've thought of
different plans and ways to stop people from littering, but
I don't think that's possible. So, I decided that I would
start picking up trash when I'm out at fishing spots or
anywhere in general. I take pleasure in picking up some
garbage. I could do more, but it's not a perfect solution. It
is taking ownership of the places I go.

There are some fishing spots that I won't go to anymore because of the trashed nature of the places. Swan Pond is one of them. McKay Lake is another. Canoe Lake. You just can't look past it.

Swan Pond was one of our favorite places, in part because of the beautiful lily pads. In fact, our first experience with Lily pads was at Swan Pond. It's hard to explain how much litter takes away from the adventure. It's like sin in some respects.

I remember one story about Secret Pond. One evening I was going up there, driving over the farm fields and up into the woods. On the side of the dirt road, someone had dumped a pickup truck full of garbage. It was such a disappointment, and it damaged my trip. It was so hard to see that there. I remember making one more trip up there. I said I'm going to have to do something about that.

I came up with my 4x8 trailer and filled it up. As I returned over the farm field, the head of Hallockville was out by the parking lot near the North Road. He flagged me down. He accused me of trying to dump garbage in the woods. I protested but to no avail.

He doesn't know me at all.

KETCHAM CREEK

I remember my father telling me stories about muskrat trapping and his father quail hunting locally with a Parker double barrel shotgun at some of the farms up north in the Amityville area. At one of the farms he hunted, he would give the fellow a pint, and he would tell grandpa where in the fields the quail were. He kept an eye out for him.

I remember the property down on the corner of Merrick and Bay View, the Crest property. They had an old boat house where my father kept his boat. It was a nice ride through the overgrown farm field to the boat house. There were mourning doves in those fields. This was the last farm field in Amityville, New York.

I remember that dad could whistle the call of a mourning dove, and they would call back. Boy did I want to be able to do that! I could hardly whistle at the time, but I was determined to be able to do that. I worked and practiced. I finally learned how to whistle a mourning dove call. When I heard the dove call back, I knew I finally had it right. It's hard to believe, but I can still make that mourning dove call sixty years later—one long tone followed by a short crisp one.

I loved the Crest property. It gave me a love for the countryside, even though it was only twenty acres. Ketchum Creek formed a small pond before it went under Merrick Road. It was a pond I would often check out as a kid. We could walk there on Lake Drive. They filled up part of it with broken concrete and sand. It had some fish in it, white perch, a big school that would run along the shoreline. I never could get them to bite. We usually fished with worms, and they didn't seem interested.

I was there one day and found an old trunk. I was paddling around the pond in it with an old board. I think I was around ten or eleven paddling around in an old trunk with the lid open. The lid stabilized it. I was surprised it didn't leak much. Those were the early days of wanting a boat.

On another trip there, I found a steel mortar tub, old and rusty but intact, on the Amityville side of the pond. It was three feet wide, about seven feet long, and eleven inches deep. That worked great as a boat. I even had a friend go in with me. I always remembered that—in case I ever needed a boat—that worked perfectly. We would go there in different seasons.

One wintertime, the pond was partially frozen, maybe twenty feet from the shore. I was there with Richie and John, boyhood friends. We were on the woods side walking along the edge, a little on the ice. John started walking out on the ice. He walked right out to the edge and the edge broke off. John was up to his neck in that freezing water. The look on his face and the panic in his voice scared me. I remember this like it was yesterday. I was running back and forth trying to figure out what to do. I was panicked. I thought I should run home and get an adult to help, but within seconds I realized that we had to do something.

As I look back on this years later, it came over me that we needed to get a branch or something to lay over there for John. So that's what I did. There just happened to be a long limb right up the woods. It really was scary. John worked his way up on the branch and finally got out. But he had a long walk home in the woods in wet clothes in the cold. He made it home safe and sound. Praise God.

One more story from Ketchum Creek. We were there one summer day fishing and exploring. I had a small spool of fishing line probably wrapped around a stick or small tree limb. I was fishing the southside of Merrick Road on Ketchum Creek with a worm. I was maybe ten years old. I had a small hook and I'm just flinging it there, no pole or reel. I started catching killies, the biggest killies I ever saw. I'd never really fished for killies before but they were biting. I remember when I swung the bait out there and would get a bite, I would pull on the line real hard and the fish would come up out of the water and land on the beach. I did that a few times. It was fun. I thought about it in later years. I've never fished that way again.

I had a ball at Ketchum Creek. I think that was the start of all my adventures. It's lasted a lifetime.

CENTER POND IN RIVERHEAD

I've been thinking about a 1990's trip to Center
Pond lately. I'm reading a book about a man who became
a Christian in jail, and it got me thinking about this pond
along 51, a route in Riverhead, New York. This pond is in
the Pine Barrens. I think it was a cranberry bog in its day.
It's very close to the road and wooded all around the sides
and in the back in an area that backs up to the Suffolk
County jail. It looked promising. There's another pond in
the area immediately adjacent to the jail fence and the
barbed wire. That pond looked even better, but I didn't
think it was worth the risk of encountering trouble. I
fished at the safer pond, Center Pond.

I stopped at Center Pond on a nice day, a little
overcast. The last time I came I caught one Pickerel. I cast
from the shoreline. This time I came with waders. I'm
donning my waders and getting the pole out of the truck.
I'm kinda excited as I usually am when I put on my waders
and grab my fishing pole. I'm feeling pretty confident. I've
been to a lot of ponds in the Pine Barrens with waders on.
It doesn't look like anybody fishes here. I'm walking in and
the bottom feels good. Not really muddy. I make a bunch
of casts and I'm moving out further in the pond. The
water is just above my knees. I'm enjoying being here. It

looks like it gets deeper at an edge in the water where it drops. I can't see the edge well. I'm walking out a little further into the pond. Making a few casts. All of a sudden, the bottom gives way. Instead of standing in water a little up to my knees, I'm suddenly immersed in water up to my chest at the top of my waders. No warning, like an elevator giving way. The water did not go over the top of my waders, though. The bottom let go. I was a little spooked. I climbed back toward the shore. I don't know what I was walking on. I didn't go back fishing there again. But as I thought on the way home, that's where the fish were hiding. Under that layer.

LOST

Psalm 19 and Col 1: 15-20

I was coming home from a morning fishing trip and pulling into Lake Redwine, when I saw a friend of mine walking/jogging as he often does. I'm looking for a plumbing part for him, one that has been difficult to find. I tell him that "I haven't given up yet, Brock." He says not to worry. He tells me about a house being built on his block on a pond that I've fished a few times. It's kind of nice. I asked him if he knew of any other ponds with little hope for a helpful answer. But he says that he does! He rode his bike to one, and he told me where it was.

I'm already getting excited—a new pond to investigate. I head home and look it up on a map. It's off why 29. They are building over there. There are no houses. It's for sale as a commercial property, a large property with a pond. I'm off to see this new pond.

I'm looking for the path that Brock took with his bike. Eventually, I find a trail. It looks good and I start walking back. The trail was quite overgrown, but clear enough to walk. I walk for about ten minutes deeper into the woods. There are nice big trees. I like it. There's a cross path where you can make a right or a left; I'm thinking I'll go right. So often I'm wrong about those instincts, so I think I should probably go left. But right looks nice, so I go right.

I walk another ten minutes. This land is a little rolling. I'm looking for the pond, but I don't see it. I follow a few more paths, but I still don't see it. Nothing. I'm lost. I can't believe that I haven't found it yet. I hear the traffic on 29. Normally I'd be disappointed to hear the traffic, but right now it's reassuring. I tell myself not to panic and to head towards the traffic noise.

So that's what I did. I started to sweat after my long hike. I came in sight of the road. It was quite a hike back to the truck. I was a little surprised that I still had not sited the pond. I was going to give up and try another day. I was tired and sweaty, but I got my phone out and looked at the GPS and there it was.

Back into the woods, but this time I followed the GPS. I kept making corrections on route. I finally came into a beautiful pond with a small beaver dam on the end. I thought, I wish I had a chair to sit awhile and enjoy all this beauty. I can still hear the road in the background.

I was thinking how often we go to Lowes to get new plants for our garden, but this garden was filled to the brim, and no one planted it but my great God.

STEVE'S PLACE

Steve Whitt runs the Colonial Inn in Pine Hill,
New York, in Ulster county which is in the Catskills, a
mountain range which consists of 150,000 acres, mostly
wooded. I first heard of Steve's place from my son's youth
group leader, Bill. He had been going up there since he
was young to ski with his family at Belleayre Mountain Ski
Center, so Bill planned trips with the youth group. Because
I love fishing, Bill would tell me about Steve's fishing all
the time. Bill didn't go to Pine Hill to fish, but he could tell
that Steve loved fishing because it was evident from the
decor which included stuffed fish and trophy mounts.
Nonetheless, I was a little doubtful of the great fishing, but
my sons prodded me, and we made a trip to Pine Hill,
New York, to visit Colonial Inn, Steve's Place, to catch
some trout.

To get to Steve's Place, you make a left off the
NY thruway at Kingston and go west 40 minutes on Route
28, around 4 hours from our home on Long Island
depending on traffic through the city. The Colonial Inn is
a big 1870 Inn with 20 rooms to rent, a big dining room, a
large lounge area, and a wraparound front porch. It's on a
narrow road on one end of a small town with a population
of less than three hundred people. All the buildings in

town are over a hundred years old. They show their age, too. The winters here can drop to 20 below zero.

The first time I went with the boys it was spring, and we were going to fish for trout. I didn't really know what to expect, but Steve's Place did not disappoint – neither did Steve. Steve is the quintessential hunter, fisherman, innkeeper, guide, and collector. This was the start of a 30-year relationship with Steve's place, and Steve, and the Catskill Mountains. It was also the beginning of a wonderful relationship with smallmouth bass; brook, brown, and rainbow trout; bears; small streams; brooks; ponds; spillways; pools; reservoirs; a private fishing club; bait fishing; and sitting on an old porch enjoying the mountains and talking with Steve in the morning over breakfast.

Steve made breakfast every morning. He'd ask you what you wanted, but we usually had French toast, scrambled eggs, and bacon. But what I remember most is Steve telling us about new fishing spots and writing the directions on napkins—directions that I could never follow, but I loved trying. Over the years to come, I did find some of Steve's "napkin" fishing spots, and I loved them. We caught a lot of fish. Steve's stories about Pulaski, New York, and his salmon fishing in the Salmon River inspired us to go there, too. The first one I caught was a thirty-pounder, all because of Steve and his wonderful stories.

CRYSTAL AND BILL

I'm reading through the New Testament again because of a Billy Graham video that challenged an atheist to read the New Testament. I'm not an atheist, but I took up the challenge anyway to see God more clearly in the scriptures, and I am. I see that I need to be here reading the gospel accounts slowly, a chapter or two a day. Reading Jesus's high priestly prayer in John five times—so much in that I'm starting to underline in the gospel verses that jump out at me. There are many:

John 1:12, Luke 24:45-47, John 9: 25,

John 10:27-30, John 14: 35, Acts 17: 2

and many more. I'm reading through Romans, one chapter at a time and reading them twice and underlining.

A person comes to mind who had her whole bible underlined in different colors. At one time, I thought you shouldn't do that kind of stuff. I learned that in grade school: "Don't write in your books!" But I am seeing it differently now.

So, Crystal came to church. She was a faithful attender. She was single, young, and a dental hygienist. She met a nice young man and got married. They both came to church, and we became good friends. Bill, her husband, was a country boy raised in Tennessee. He got into the air conditioner business and was out trying to make a living. He was a hard worker and diligent. He got a contract with a local gas station owner who owned something like a hundred gas stations in the greater New York area. He knew that Bill was the guy to hire.

Bill loved fishing and ate the fish he caught. He especially loved Bluegills and Sunnies. They call them Brim in Georgia. Bill had all the equipment to fillet and deep fat fry them. I had never eaten one before, but I have caught tons of them. We made a date to go fishing and go back to the house and cook them.

There's a small pond on Sill's Lane in rural Southold that runs along a railroad track, a third of a mile from a parking spot. The train comes just twice a day, so Bill, Crystal, and I walked along the tracks. It was in the evening and a nice walk along the tree lined tracks. We set up right along the track on the west side of the pond using worms and jig heads.

Bill is a seasoned fishing person; Crystal not at all. We started catching nice bluegills, and we were catching some every cast. We didn't move from that spot. It wasn't long before we had a pail full. I'm always anxious to bring people fishing. What if we don't catch any fish, and they are disappointed? I've brought others to this spot and always caught fish, so we had a successful trip.

171

We went home and Bill fileted the pail of Bluegill and plugged the fryer in. He deep fried a mess of bluegills. I remember Jacki asking Crystal, "How was the fishing," and Crystal answered, "I caught one every cast." I thought, "now that was good fishing trip!" This was some ten years ago and was brought to my mind because of underlining scripture in my Bible. I miss Bill and Crystal.

BUCK AND NORA

I had an old friend and his wife over for a visit. I
haven't seen them personally for twenty-five years. The
fact that the Brieds were coming to visit got me thinking
about the past. I think a word that Mrs. Jackson wrote on
the first page of this writing book "Reflections" is so good
because they come like that — reflections sending me back
to a time long ago. It was like the letter from the fire
department that Ken Lang sent. It turns the channel back
a long time. It hasn't really done that in such a broad and
expansive way. As I write these stories, things start
coming. Some are very pleasant to remember, some not so
pleasant. This one makes me smile.

Buck and Nora were friends of Joe Slack, an
Amityville person. He was a bread-delivery man, tree man,
coon hunter, dog lover, and a tough guy. This story, and
there are quite a few with Joe, was in the 1960s when I was
in my teens. Joe sold firewood and had a spot to get some
in Manorville, New York. This was one of my first jobs
with Joe. We were headed out east to the Navy Grumman
property in the pine barrens. It is the largest vacant land on
Long Island.

It was a long ride there, at least an hour, in a 1947
Dodge Rack Truck with no front seats. We sat on 5-gallon

paint buckets, but we made it there okay. The truck was hard to start. You had to pull the choke out, and Joe struggled with it.

On this trip, the goal was to get firewood and to help Joe clear some paths. I was just a laborer. I think the intention was to clear it out enough to create a shooting game preserve or to just open it up more. It was on 35-acres. There was nothing else around.

The two people in charge of the property were Buck and his wife, Nora. They seemed elderly to me. I think they were from down south, maybe Louisiana. It looked like they'd led a rough life. They had wrinkles and rough hands from working. They were nice people. They had a goose that would chase you. You had to be careful. I remember that it got late, and Nora invited me and Joe to have dinner. She had a pot of something on the stove. Joe was happy about that.

At the time, I was a very fussy eater. If something looked funny, I could not eat it. I was weary about that pot on the stove in their trailer on the other side of the street from the property.

We sat at the table with a bowl of *something*. I was trying to eat it. It was very difficult. I remember looking in the bowl, and I was sure there were eyeballs floating around.

I started gagging, but I didn't want to be disrespectful. Joe was just slopping it all down. Then he says in a loud voice, "Can I have another bowl?"

I was mumbling, "I'm not hungry, and I'm not feeling well," hoping to get out of there—and Joe wants more. This was the beginning of a lot of adventures with Joe Slack.

I never found out what was in the bowl.

EVAN

We are going to Southold to spend some time
with Katherine, Jonathan, Evan, and Vivienne. We haven't
been back since we moved to Georgia six years ago.
Katherine is renting a house on Great Pond. Wow! I'm
going fishing on Great Pond again with Evan and
Vivienne. Katherine said Evan wanted to catch a
largemouth bass. I think back to when Tom, Sean, and I
caught our first largemouth bass at Great Pond and all the
other fish we caught there. It's a special place for us. I
learned so much there about fishing. Over the time we
spent there, we learned so much about different species of
fish, different baits, poles, and reels. We used to get the
Bass Pro Shop catalog, pour it over it, and order things.
We'd put them to use on Great Pond.

We saw so much wildlife there: turtles, hawks,
muskrats, owls, fish chasing our baits. It really holds so
many memories, especially time spent with my boys.
Another generation is coming to fish for largemouth bass
at Great Pond—Evan.

As I first thought about going fishing with my
grandson, I thought I sure want to put him on the fish and
catch a bunch! I want to be with Evan and talk and be
together while fishing. I have memories of taking people

fishing and being anxious that they weren't going to catch anything. You can't foresee what's going to happen, but I know it's going to be an adventure.

I was also thinking about other places we could go. There's a lot of them. It's possible that we could go walk on the Long Island Sound with a fishing pole and make a few casts. We could walk for miles. Maybe we could go to Orient Point, Laurel Lake, or that pond on Main Bay View Road that always had a bunch of bass in it. Maybe we could visit the Railroad Tressel in the evening and fish there. Maybe the pond in Greenport by the railroad tracks. Maybe we could get a few clams. It's a big list, but I'm hoping Great Pond will be so fishy that we won't be thinking about another place to go.

Evan—Grandpa can't wait to go fishing and spend time with you!

And maybe hold Vivienne's hand and walk along the Long Island Sound and find some nice shells on her birthday.

CROOKED POND, EAST HAMPTON

I think about writing all these fishing stories. I came to a title on the top of a page that I wanted to write about. I just passed it by. As I'm trying to close out my memoirs, which is harder than I thought – there's a lot to writing a book – I've got to keep checking the spelling and structure and word choice. As I'm doing this I have a title on the page – Green Eyed Monster, East Hampton in the 90s.

It was a pond on the Southside, Joe's neighborhood. It's one of our earliest fishing trips with Joe Russo. There have been many since. He's a good fishing buddy. The boys love Joe and love going fishing with him and have on many occasions. On this trip to Crooked Pond, we were looking to catch some bass. We all did.

One of the humorous things about this trip was that Joe had a bait called a Green-Eyed Monster. We were all laughing at it, and Joe was making jokes about it, too. He even hooked it up funny on the hook, too. We were all getting a kick out of it. It didn't deter Joe one bit. He cast it around, and low and behold, Joe reels in a three-pound bass on a Green-Eyed Monster hooked crooked.

Joe would bring that up when we fished in other places—there were many. Every now and then, Joe hooked his bait crooked and brought up that time he caught a three-pound bass on the Green-Eyed Monster.

A MORNING WALK

I try to walk three days a week weather permitting. In the fall, especially this fall, it's a pleasure to take walks. I start on Lake Redwine Plantation Drive and head up to the front of Lake Redwine. I only have words to describe what I experienced today, but I will try to do it some justice.

On fall mornings, the lower angle of the sun slices through the leaves and glistens so that the colors—yellow, red, orange, and all shades of brown—are truly extraordinary. I'm very appreciative of those colors and the sunlight on my morning walks!

The beautiful mornings remind me how incredible God's creation is. The turning leaves are like Fall's flowers, and I have eyes to see them and appreciate them. Praise God! I'm up to the South Shore in Lake Redwine just enjoying my walk when I notice the leaves falling—the different shapes and colors. They fall in different patterns. Some floating, some dive bombing, some spiraling, and some like drill bits turning. It's happening all around me with the morning sun reflecting and streaming through the leaves coming down. It's raining leaves.

I had to stop and just wait on the spectacle of leaves. I needed a chair just to sit and watch. It was like a parade of leaves. I tried to watch each of the leaves fall and how they sailed. It's a fall wonderland. It's all around me. I can hear them, the rustling. All my senses are ringing. I'm overcome by the beauty of it all. Is this really happening on Redwine Plantation Drive? It was hard to take it all in. I don't think I did, but I had to try. It was *a happening* in nature, and there are many. This I was blessed to see — this spectacular show only two blocks away from my house. And I was the only one there to experience it.

In his sermon "The Weight of Glory," C.S. Lewis observed that "We do not want merely to see beauty... we want something else which can hardly be put into words— to be united with the beauty we see, to pass into it, to receive it into ourselves, to bathe in it, to become part of it." Yes, that's what I'm looking for. In a small way, I did that this morning on my fall walk through Fall's flowers.

In every season, there is something happening— some glory to behold, to cherish, and to praise.

EPILOGUE
March 26, 2024

I have to say, as I end this project of writing my memoirs, in a lot of ways it's a new beginning. I'm seeing things differently. I always liked nature, creation, but I'm looking at it differently now. Especially flowers. Nature is a screen loosely hiding an omnipresent God, as Emerson called it a veil to the eternal. And as Psalm 19 reports, "the heavens declare the glory of God and his handiwork. It speaks and uses no words, but everyone hears."

It wasn't what I was thinking about when I started this journey in writing. I've often had to call myself back to my original intent to write my life stories for my Toot and family. At times, it was like a clogged drain just dripping through memories. Until it broke through and memories came flooding in. There are so many at times. And occasionally they were so emotional that I would weep reading them from my journal to Mrs. Jackson as she typed them for me. I'm getting better at that, but still....

I couldn't really remember anything about my father until the story about splitting wood for him. After that, so many more stories about him filtered back into my mind. I know there were things in my past that I don't care to remember or to tell, but there are so many good ones that I am taken aback by how many. They still keep coming.

As I've been thinking about this, I am mindful of how good God has been to me. He hasn't treated me according to my sins, or as my sins deserved. He is a good God, a merciful God, a kind God, a loving God. I think of the words of "It is Well with my Soul" often: "My sin – oh the bliss of this glorious thought, my sin, not in part, but the whole, is nailed to the cross, and I bear it no more. Praise the lord, praise the lord, Oh My Soul."

So, this small book I've been working on brought me places and showed me things I could not have imagined when I started it. Praise God from whom all blessings flow.

Made in United States
Orlando, FL
09 September 2024